PLUNDER?

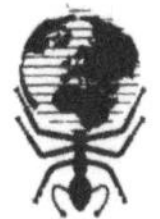

PLUNDER?

HOW MUSEUMS GOT THEIR TREASURES

Justin M. Jacobs

REAKTION BOOKS

To my parents, for always encouraging and supporting my education, wherever it took me

Published by
REAKTION BOOKS LTD
2–4 Sebastian Street
London EC1V 0HE, UK
www.reaktionbooks.co.uk

First published 2024
First published in paperback 2025

EU GPSR Authorised Representative
Logos Europe, 9 rue Nicolas Poussin, 17000, La Rochelle, France
email: contact@logoseurope.eu

Printed and bound in Great Britain by TJ Books, Padstow, Cornwall

A catalogue record for this book is available from the British Library

ISBN 978 1 83639 108 1

CONTENTS

INTRODUCTION

On 6 January 2021, an angry mob stormed the U.S. Capitol Building in Washington, DC, and left a trail of devastation in its wake. Out of the many shocking images to emerge from that day, perhaps one of the most widely circulated was the photograph of a man, his face tinged with red paint and sporting a Cheshire cat grin, carrying the lectern of House Speaker Nancy Pelosi across the main rotunda. It quickly spread as a meme on social media, modified in humorous ways to suit various audiences. One particular version caught my eye on Twitter. It included the following caption just below the lectern: '19th-century Western archaeologists'. The message was clear, concise and clever: in removing so many ancient artefacts to European and American museums over the past several centuries, Western archaeologists had behaved no better than the Capitol riot mob. What happened to Pelosi's lectern was the same thing that had happened to the Elgin Marbles, the Benin Bronzes and Priam's Treasure.

Of course, Internet memes are two a penny, and one should perhaps not read too deeply into such fleeting ephemera. But in this particular case, a hastily cobbled social media post – originally designed to elicit nothing more than a brief laugh and a quick scoff – did indeed succeed in capturing the cultural zeitgeist of our age.

To find evidence of this, one need look no further than your local bookshop, where explosive words like 'rape', 'plunder' or 'loot' appear in the titles of any number of books on archaeology and museums published in the past several decades: *The Rape of the Nile* (1975), *The Rape of Egypt* (1991), *The Rape of Tutankhamun* (1993), *The Rape of Europa* (1995), *The Great American Plunder of Persia's Antiquities* (2003), *The Medici Conspiracy: The Illicit Journey of Looted Antiquities* (2006), *Loot: The Battle over the Stolen Treasures of the Ancient World* (2008), *Chasing Aphrodite: The Hunt for Looted Antiquities at the World's Richest Museum* (2011), *Loot: Britain and the Benin Bronzes* (2021) and *Plunder: Napoleon's Theft of Veronese's Feast* (2021).

The assumptions embedded in these titles are not subtle, to say the least. In short, any time a work of art or an ancient artefact is removed from the land in which it was produced, that act of removal is considered morally repugnant – on a par with rape. This idea, once confined to narrow academic debates, has in recent years vaulted into mainstream consciousness. No book better illustrates this conceptual leap than Dan Hicks's indignantly titled *The Brutish Museums: The Benin Bronzes, Colonial Violence and Cultural Restitution* (2020). On the book jacket, readers are told in no uncertain terms that if they have ever visited a museum before, then they have effectively walked through a crime scene:

> Walk into any Western museum today and you will see the curated spoils of Empire. They sit behind plate glass: dignified, tastefully lit. Accompanying pieces of card offer a name, date and place of origin. They do not mention that the objects are all stolen.

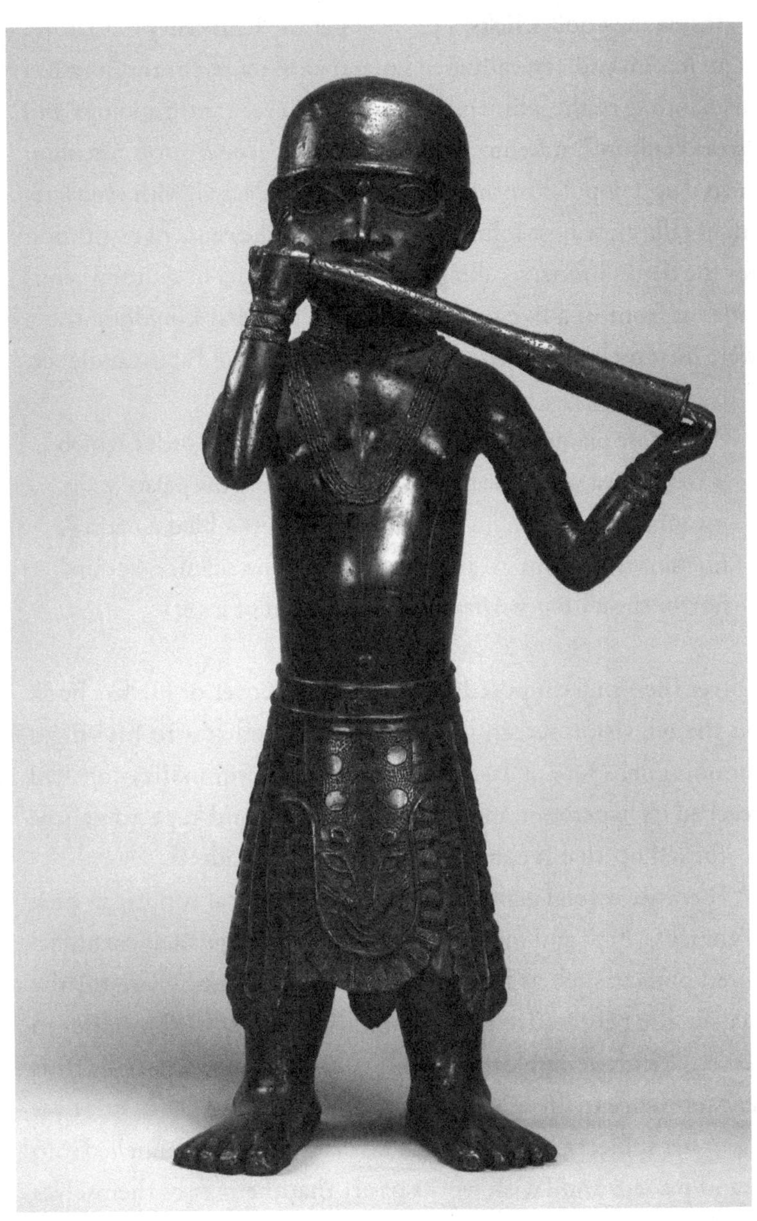

Benin Bronze artefact at the Metropolitan Museum of Art, New York.

Inside the book, Hicks, a professor at the University of Oxford, is no less incendiary, calling in unequivocal terms for the 'physical dismantling of the white infrastructure of every anthropology and "world culture" museum' across the planet.[1] *The Brutish Museums* stirred up a popular storm when it was first released, with even late-night talk show host John Oliver taking up the cause of restitution for the Benin Bronzes, calling their removal an act of 'cultural genocide' in front of a live studio audience. 'For that kingdom, these were their memories made physical,' Oliver shouted at his audience.

> And these plaques were laid out in a very specific order, which was then lost when the British tore them from the palace walls, meaning the British, in effect, stole and scrambled a nation's memories, a crime so fucked up even [the science-fiction/horror show] *Black Mirror* hasn't thought of it yet.

Oliver then superimposed an image of the cover of Hicks's book on the television screen to lend academic gravitas to his vulgar monologue. Here at last the discourse of criminalization had reached its hyperbolic apogee: from 'plunder' and 'rape' to a crime so 'fucked up' that it constituted 'cultural genocide'.[2]

There are several glaring omissions of historical context in such arguments. First and foremost is the fact that exquisitely manufactured objects such as the Benin Bronzes were not made for the masses, the people. They were commissioned by wealthy elites to serve as exclusive emblems of political power and social status. This lent substance to the monarch's jealously guarded right to rule over his or her subjects, whose labour and taxes would be funnelled into grand palaces and lavish works of art that the masses themselves would never get to see or enjoy. The Benin Bronzes, much like the extravagant collection of Chinese bronzes, porcelains and paintings stored in the Forbidden City, were not originally regarded as symbols of any nation, nor did they tell that nation's 'story'. If they told any story at all, it was one that extolled the character, taste and rule of the haughty kings and emperors who jealously hoarded them – and of the gods who supposedly blessed them. If any one of the vast majority of people who comprised the Nigerian or Chinese 'nations' of the day had attempted to sneak a peek at the Benin or Chinese bronzes, they would have quickly lost their head. After all, the Forbidden City was not an idle name: it, and all the art and architecture inside it, was quite literally forbidden to anyone other than the emperor and whomsoever he chose to share it with. Taken together, those people who could actually view and touch the treasures of the Forbidden City constituted an infinitesimal percentage of the population.

But there is an even bigger problem with the criminalizing discourse of modern cultural polemics, one that goes far beyond the mere lack of historical context or nuance. And that problem is this: regardless of whether the Benin Bronzes represented the inclusive memories of the Nigerian nation or were vain, self-congratulatory indulgences of the Benin elites, the method of their removal from Africa to Europe was merely one out of many. And this particular method – military plunder – was highly irregular and decidedly unrepresentative of how most artefacts and artwork from the non-Western world found their way into Western museums. Military plunder involved hundreds or thousands of armed men, acting on orders from their superiors, shooting their way across the land in an attempt to break into a palace or fortress with the explicit intent to maim and kill anyone who got in their way. If the soldiers happened to survive all this carnage, blood-stained loot was one of their rewards.

Military plunder is easy to criticize. But it was not the norm. Museums do not maintain, nor have they ever maintained, standing armies. Their institutional strengths are to be found in their purses, which are filled by wealthy donors and government coffers. The foot soldiers who actually carried out plunder in distant lands – poorly educated young men drawn from less privileged sectors of society – were rarely inclined to donate their hard-fought spoils of war to any institution without financial compensation. So in most cases, whenever a Western museum acquired objects looted by Western armies, it did so not by ordering its 'armies' to hand them over, but by writing a cheque – if not to the soldier who physically looted them, then to the wealthier collector, dealer or auction house who first bought them from him.

To sceptical readers, this may seem like a small and meaningless distinction. So what if museums merely paid someone else to acquire their morally tainted goods? Doesn't that make them the institutional equivalent of a person who hires a hitman to carry out a murder? With specific regard to military plunder, the answer is yes – they are indeed morally equivalent. But once we acknowledge the obvious yet overlooked fact that museums themselves did not send armies overseas, it forces us to pay closer attention to the sorts of vendors from whom museums purchased their collections.

The curators who worked in Western museums did not personally transport the objects under their care. It is more accurate to say that they purchased them. And soldiers and generals were merely one of several different types of suppliers to whom they made payment. To put this particular supplier – the soldier – into perspective, consider the fact that the British Museum contains around 8 million objects in its collection. Of those 8 million objects, just under two hundred consist of bronze plaques taken by British soldiers during their bombardment of the Benin Kingdom in 1897.[3] This comes out at 0.000024 per cent of the total collection. Even if we assume that every British military adventure during the imperial era resulted in similar amounts of plundered loot, all of it combined would still constitute a mere drop in the museum bucket.

So where did the lion's share of any given museum collection come from? Who else, besides gun-toting infantrymen, got a fat cheque for their exquisite wares? A few examples may help to place the Benin Bronzes into proper relief. When the Hungarian-born British archaeologist Aurel Stein organized an expedition to the north-western desert regions of the Qing Empire in 1906, he succeeded in gaining access to a hidden 'cave library' (although it was more a storage room than an actual library) near the oasis of Dunhuang. Sealed at some point during the early eleventh century and then forgotten about for the next nine hundred years, this hidden alcove – now known as Cave 17 – yielded more than 40,000 ancient manuscripts and paintings. Stein managed to bring fewer than 10,000 of them back with him to England. And this was the spoils from merely a single site on one of Stein's many expeditions. Many other Western scholars also brought back thousands of scrolls from Cave 17, including the French sinologist Paul Pelliot, who matched Stein's total just one year later. And when Stein returned to the abandoned oases of the Taklamakan Desert again in 1913 to collect even more ancient Buddhist antiquities, his total haul was so large it had to be expressed in weight rather than objects: 7,250 kilograms – that is, 16,000 pounds! That's more than 7 tonnes of so-called 'loot', and none of it heavy bronze plaques. But even 'heavy loot' must contend with the ultimate gold standard: when Lord Elgin brought his marbles from Greece to London and put them on display in 1807, they tipped the scales at a whopping 109 tonnes (240,300 lb).

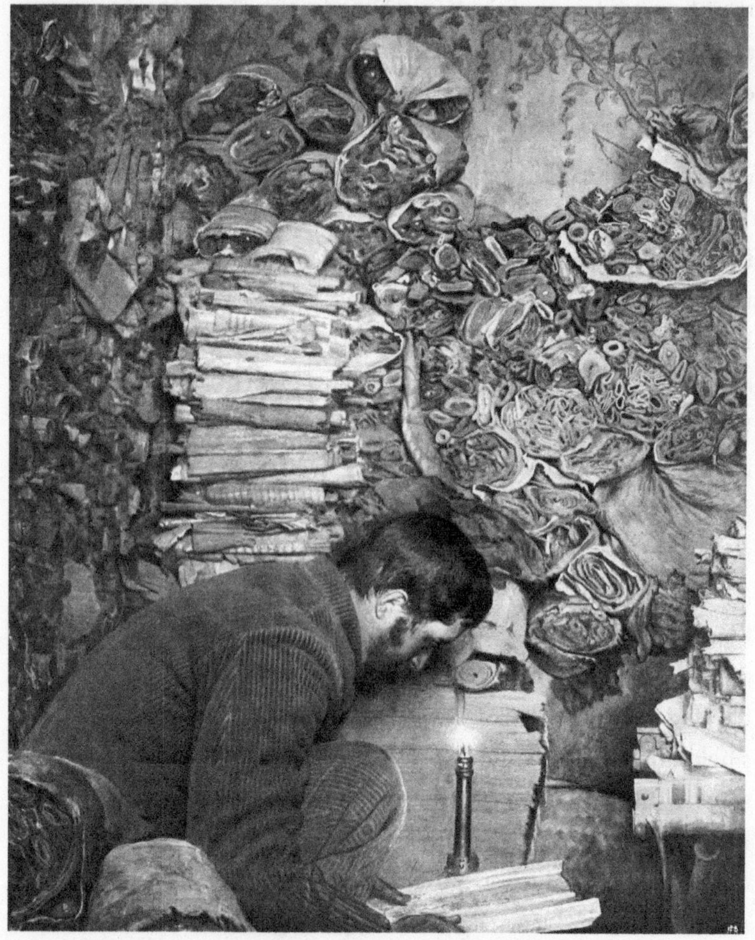

Paul Pelliot examining 40,000 manuscripts in Cave 17, Mogao Grottoes, China, 1908, photograph by Charles Nouette.

Neither Stein nor Elgin acquired these future museum objects in a manner that could be described as military plunder. Though Stein did carry firearms, they were intended to guard against possible bandits in remote desert regions. As it turned out, Stein used them only to hunt game. Lord Elgin, for his part, was unarmed, as any gentleman diplomat should be. Not only this, but he was in fact the flesh-and-blood embodiment of Great Britain's military alliance with the Ottoman sultan against the French Navy in the Mediterranean. As British ambassador to the Sublime Porte in Constantinople, Elgin was the political liaison through which Ottoman gratitude for the recapture of their Egyptian province from Napoleon would be expressed. And that gratitude came in the form of permission – both written and oral – to remove ancient Greek sculptures from the Parthenon in Athens. Another way of making sense of all this is to say that the Benin Bronzes were acquired by military plunder, the Parthenon sculptures by diplomatic gift and the lost manuscripts of Dunhuang by mobile expedition.

And the list goes on. Consider, for instance, the much celebrated tomb of the boy pharaoh Tutankhamun, discovered by the British

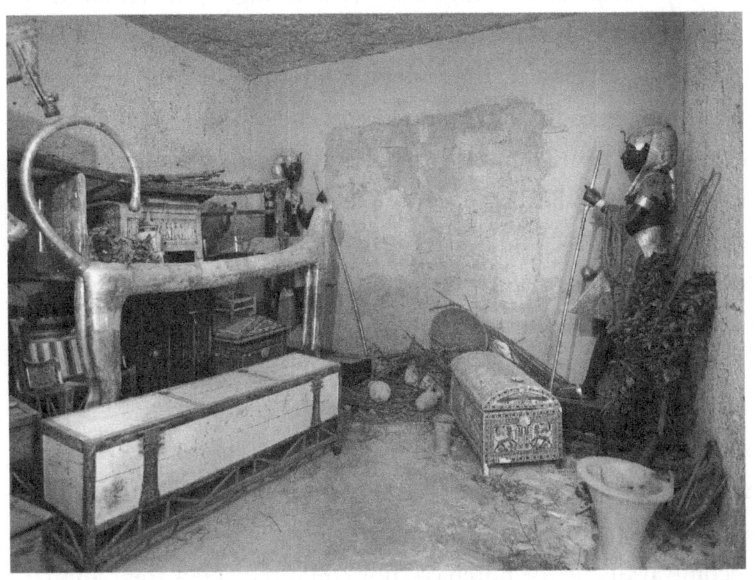

Some of the 4,000 artefacts found in Tutankhamun's tomb, 1922, photograph by Harry Burton.

archaeologist Howard Carter in November 1922 in the Valley of the Kings in Egypt. By the time Carter finished his survey of its densely packed treasures, the catalogue included more than 4,000 objects. Though nearly all of them ended up in the National Museum in Cairo rather than in the British Museum in London or the Metropolitan Museum in New York – as Carter's wealthy patron, Lord Carnarvon, originally planned – their sheer number still gives us a sense of just how many museum artefacts could be found in countless ancient tombs across the globe, even if they had not escaped (as had Tut's tomb) the covetous hands of ancient tomb robbers. Regardless, royal tombs like those found in the Valley of the Kings tended to be located far from major population centres – and thus quite remote from the intended victims of marauding armies. Not surprisingly then, Carter's work in the Valley of the Kings, and that of every foreign archaeologist before him, highlights yet another category of acquisition: stationary excavations.

Last but not least are the dealers. While museums may be willing to write cheques to soldiers, diplomats and scholars, such vendors are relatively few in number (even if the collections of the latter two may occasionally be disproportionately large). Far more ubiquitous are the networks of antiquities dealers. Easily the least studied and most poorly understood of all potential vendors that museums dealt with, dealers were almost certainly responsible for the vast majority of objects that you can see in most major museums around the world today. This is due to the fact that they were easy to do business with and as numerous as flies. By contrast, the spoils of military plunder and diplomatic gifts appeared only intermittently and without much warning – curators could not anticipate when such objects would become available for purchase, nor could they craft their annual budgets and exhibitions around their unexpected arrival. The mobile expeditions and stationary excavations of scholars were likewise filled with uncertainty. When the director of a museum in England decided to invest thousands of pounds in such an enterprise, he was taking the same risk as a gambler in a casino. Certainly, Howard Carter *might* find a lavishly stocked ancient Egyptian tomb. But it was far more likely that he would find nothing at all – as indeed was the case in each of the five fruitless years he had been digging in the Valley of the Kings before his big stroke of luck. The same calculus held for Stein's expeditions: sure, he *might* return with 10,000 ancient manuscripts. But it was just as likely that he would come home with a lacklustre collection of broken bodhisattva heads of no particular artistic merit.

By contrast, dealers were businessmen. And the success of their business depended primarily on securing a reliable supply of goods to sell to museums on the basis of mutually recognized valuations established by past precedent. Not only that, but dealers could also fulfil commissions for specific objects 'on demand', so to speak, in order to fill in the gaps of a particular collection. In other words, dealers were predictable, reliable and pliable – three traits that made them irresistible vendors for museums. As a result, according to Egyptologists Fredrik Hagen and Kim Ryholt, 'most Egyptian objects in Western museums have been purchased rather than excavated.'[4] This despite the long-standing popular fascination with archaeologists such as Howard Carter and his less rigorous but more dashing forebear Giovanni Belzoni. In other words, stationary excavations, mobile expeditions and military plunder get all the attention because they make for compelling, easily comprehensible stories. The agents of good and evil are always easy to identify. In the earliest tellings, brave soldiers defending their nation's honour sailed to far-off lands to teach indulgent Chinese mandarins a lesson and punish dark-skinned savages in the African jungle for their treachery. Somewhat less violently, heroic men of science endured frostbite and blazing deserts to rescue neglected and misunderstood ancient treasures from ignorant natives.

Now, of course, new generations of storytellers have flipped these roles on their head. We now hear tell of smug white soldiers who brutalized oppressed colonial peoples in bloody pursuit of imperial loot and of racist scholars who manipulated the supposedly altruistic discourse of science as a perverted cover for their imperialist schemes of native disenfranchisement. This new set of stories is just as simplistic and dismissive of historical nuance as the self-serving narratives they aim to replace. Worst of all, they make virtually no allowance for the recognition of crucial distinctions among different means of artefact acquisition: as the discourse surrounding the Benin Bronzes clearly shows, everything in a museum is now regarded as stolen and equated with cultural rape and genocide. Soldiers, dealers, diplomats or scholars – what difference does it make? They were all imperialist thieves regardless. Ten thousand manuscripts or two hundred bronzes – who cares? It's all the stolen memories of oppressed nations anyway.

As a historian who has studied museums and archaeological expeditions for more than two decades, I find these Manichaean stories of light versus dark to be exasperating. In our desire to project meaning onto a complex subject, we have repeatedly told simplistic bedtime stories about how museums got their treasures. The heroic Western man of science was little more than a self-serving caricature. So too is the evil imperialist villain. Both projections are more suitable for a comic book than for intelligent public discourse. What is lost in all of these bold, uncompromising narratives are the words and actions of the many non-Western people who engaged the foreign collectors at the time they were removing antiquities from their lands. Strident calls for repatriation from the king of Nigeria today tell us no more about the original historical context in which the Benin Bronzes left the Benin Kingdom over a century ago than do the defensive rationalizations of museum curators who reject demands to hand over their collections in the present day.

Can anyone truly speak on behalf of ancestors – literal or figurative – who lived four, five, or even ten generations ago? In 1985 the historian David Lowenthal published a book titled *The Past Is a Foreign Country*, a now classic study of how we humans constantly rework the heritage of past generations for new purposes in the present wholly unanticipated by our forebears. 'The past is a foreign country,' I often tell my students. 'They do things differently there.' As a historian, I never cease to be surprised at what people in the past believed, said and did. We approach the past with preconceived notions modelled on our own unique experiences, only to find that the equally unique conditions of a different day and age produced behaviours of a different sort that are hard to comprehend today. If this is the case with our own ancestors, how much more so with people who lived centuries ago in lands halfway across the globe?

And yet most of us have little compunction in speaking on behalf of long-dead Egyptians, Persians and Chinese people. We imagine, with little to no historical evidence, that they must have shared the same sort of views that we hold today. Surely they regarded strange-looking foreigners from a distant land as invaders who must be resisted at all costs? Surely the Chinese regarded Stein as a thief for taking so many manuscripts from Dunhuang? In making such assumptions, however, we end up appropriating the already marginalized voices of silent historical actors. Much like John Oliver on his late-night talk show, we habitually speak on behalf of dead people, deploying their ventriloquized voices for present-day debates that would have made little sense to them during their own lifetimes. I believe that we need a new approach, one that does not speak on behalf of dead people, but rather lets dead people speak for themselves.

Let us call this the historical approach. It is an approach that views the past as if it were an elaborately worded will. The language is confusing and impenetrable to laymen, filled with specialized vocabulary and odd grammatical turns of phrase. But with the training of a professional lawyer, or in our case a professional historian – preferably one who can actually read a non-Western language, in my case Chinese – we can succeed in divining the original intent and wishes of the person who left the will, in our case those non-Western historical actors who actually engaged Western collectors in their own lifetime rather than in our present-day imagination. And in history as in wills, the feelings of the deceased do not always align with the desires of heirs. We must be prepared to accept what they tell us about why they did what they did.

In the following chapters, we will see, to the extent possible, what the people engaged in the laborious and often expensive work of transporting antiquities to distant lands thought about their role in the endeavour. Privileged white men will have their say, as they often do, but so too will illiterate Egyptian peasants, secretive Chinese dealers and hardy Uyghur guides. Sometimes they will speak directly to us in their own unmediated voices, and sometimes they will speak to us indirectly through a careful parsing of the written observations of the educated native and Western elites who interacted with them. Regardless of how their voices are recovered, it will not take long for us to discover just how differently our ancestors thought about the ownership of art and antiquities compared to how we think about it today – if they even thought about it at all.

We will examine the five major methods by which non-Western works of art made their way into Western museums or other public sites of display: military plunder, diplomatic gifts, antiquities dealers, stationary excavations and mobile expeditions. We will begin with military plunder and diplomatic gifts, because these practices have the longest historical pedigree and shared some surprising similarities. Dealers – elusive, controversial and grossly understudied – will occupy our attention next, as we attempt to understand the enormous grey area in which the vast majority of artefacts made their way into museums. Finally, we will conclude with an analysis of stationary excavations and mobile expeditions, which constitute the latest and most novel approach to the business of antiquity collecting – and, by most moral standards, its least reprehensible.

By the end of this book, I hope you will have gained a fuller appreciation of the many complex routes and motivations that were responsible for the dizzying array of objects you see the next time you enter a museum. Some of them are indeed stolen – by any definition. But most of them are not – at least by most definitions. I hope one thing above all else, however, will become clear: the origins of everything you see inside a glass cabinet or on a white pedestal deserve far more careful consideration than the parameters of our current polarized public debate have allowed thus far.

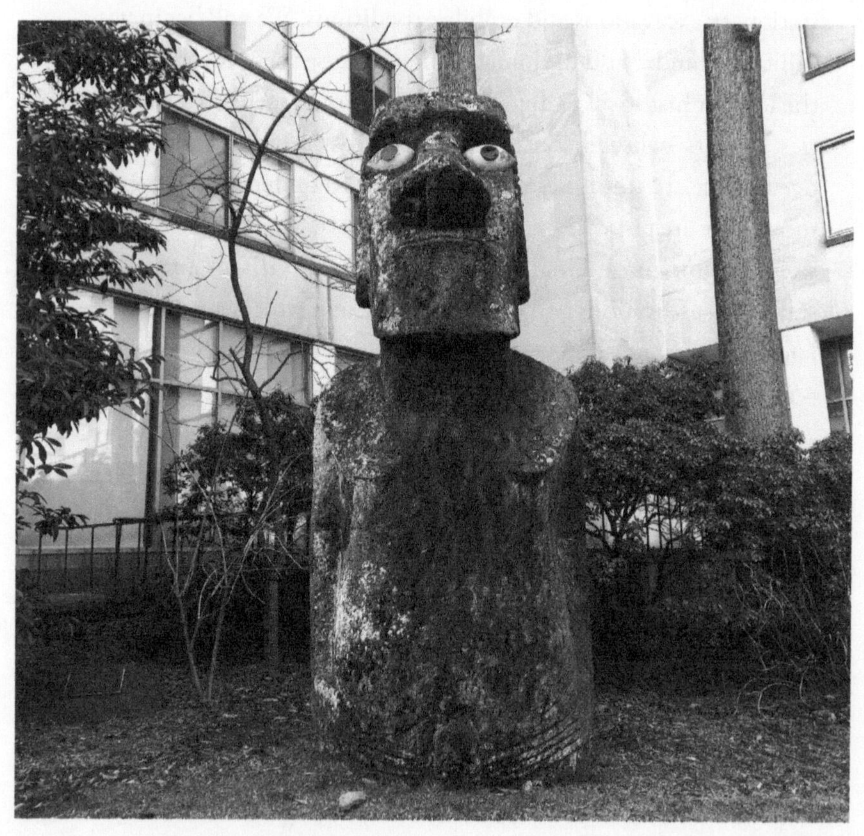

Moai replica statue at American University, Washington, DC.

1

PRESENTS AND PLUNDER

Not long ago, while walking across my university campus in Washington, DC, I nearly bumped into a 9-foot-tall stone statue. Due to my familiarity with Captain Cook's voyages in the Pacific, I instantly recognized it. It was a moai: a highly stylized representation of a powerful ancestor that can be found in many different forms throughout the Pacific Ocean on islands originally colonized by intrepid Polynesian wayfinders over a thousand years ago. Those erected on Easter Island, which were carved out of a soft volcanic rock known as tuff, are by far the largest and the most impressive. As such, they have inspired a bewildering number of theories over the years about what they can tell us about this remote island's history, from narratives of ecological collapse to alien intervention. Not immune to the moai curiosity bug, I found myself asking a very similar question. Namely, how in the world did a 9-foot-tall, multi-tonne megalith manage to find its way to an urban university campus in the United States's capital?

The answer was surprisingly hard to obtain. A small plaque embedded into a rock near the statue's base, engraved with the date of 7 June 2000, described it in vague terms as a 'gift of friendship' from Chile – which annexed Easter Island in 1888 – to American University (AU). But it said nothing about why the gift was made, who carved the moai or when. Unable to think of any reason why the university would have been the recipient of such a massive gift, I started to do some research. Unfortunately, neither the campus archives nor the campus museum had any records regarding the statue's origins. It was only during a casual conversation with a colleague over coffee that I learned of a new potential lead: the former dean of the School of International Service, now retired, possibly knew something.

One email later and the mystery was solved. The moai was a modern replica carved by native islanders that was shipped to New York for inclusion in an exhibit at the American Museum of Natural History. Once the exhibit was over, Chilean authorities were faced with a dilemma: shipping it back to Easter Island (or even Chile) would incur significant expense, but leaving it in America would require the discovery of a willing custodian – and few museums had any interest in owning a mere replica. So the Chilean ambassador picked up the phone and got in touch with an old friend of his, the dean of AU's law school, and he was all too happy to facilitate discussions with the college president over the statue. Before long, the impressive moai replica was installed on campus, with the dedication ceremony touting AU's 'global orientation and large international student' body as a rhetorical backdrop for the installation ceremony.

Although the AU moai statue is a modern replica that crossed international waters less than three decades ago, the story of its arrival on a university campus in the USA's capital is remarkably similar to those of so many other works of antiquity that made similar journeys to Western museums over the past several centuries. In short, it is representative of the first category of antiquity transfers in our list: diplomatic gifts. Along with military plunder, diplomatic gifts have an unmatched pedigree in the annals of history. In a sense, presents and plunder are flip sides of the same coin: one the result of politics gone well, the other the result of politics gone bad. In forming a moral judgement about presents and plunder, however, it is imperative that we make clear distinctions between these two forms of transfer. One is undertaken voluntarily and often with great enthusiasm, while the other involves coercion and force.

Most students and faculty at AU have never seen or heard about the moai on campus, since it is tucked away in a grassy alcove wedged in between McDowell and Hughes halls. But it is hard to miss its authentic counterpart in the British Museum, which stands alone on a square pedestal in the middle of Room 24 on the main floor, just past the gift shop. Known as Hoa Hakananai'a, it is one of two moai held by the museum. Moai Hava, its more squat and weathered companion, spends most of its days either in storage or on loan to other British museums. Both statues were removed from Easter Island by the naval crew of HMS *Topaze* in November 1868. As we will see, the story of their removal bears a fundamental resemblance with the AU replica, one that marks both statues as a textbook example of a diplomatic gift.

HMS *Topaze* was sent into South Pacific seas in the late 1860s on a surveying mission. According to Jo Anne Van Tilburg, an expert on Easter Island and author of the most in-depth study of the removal of the two moai in 1868, the crew of the *Topaze* was directed to 'verify the island's position on Admiralty charts, to search for other islands reputed to be in the vicinity, and to survey' Easter Island.[1] Among all the documentation that has survived from this voyage, there is no evidence that the expedition was organized with the prior intent of obtaining a moai statue for the British Museum. This lack of premeditation was common with diplomatic gifts, and to a lesser extent even with military plunder. Men and resources were mobilized to carry

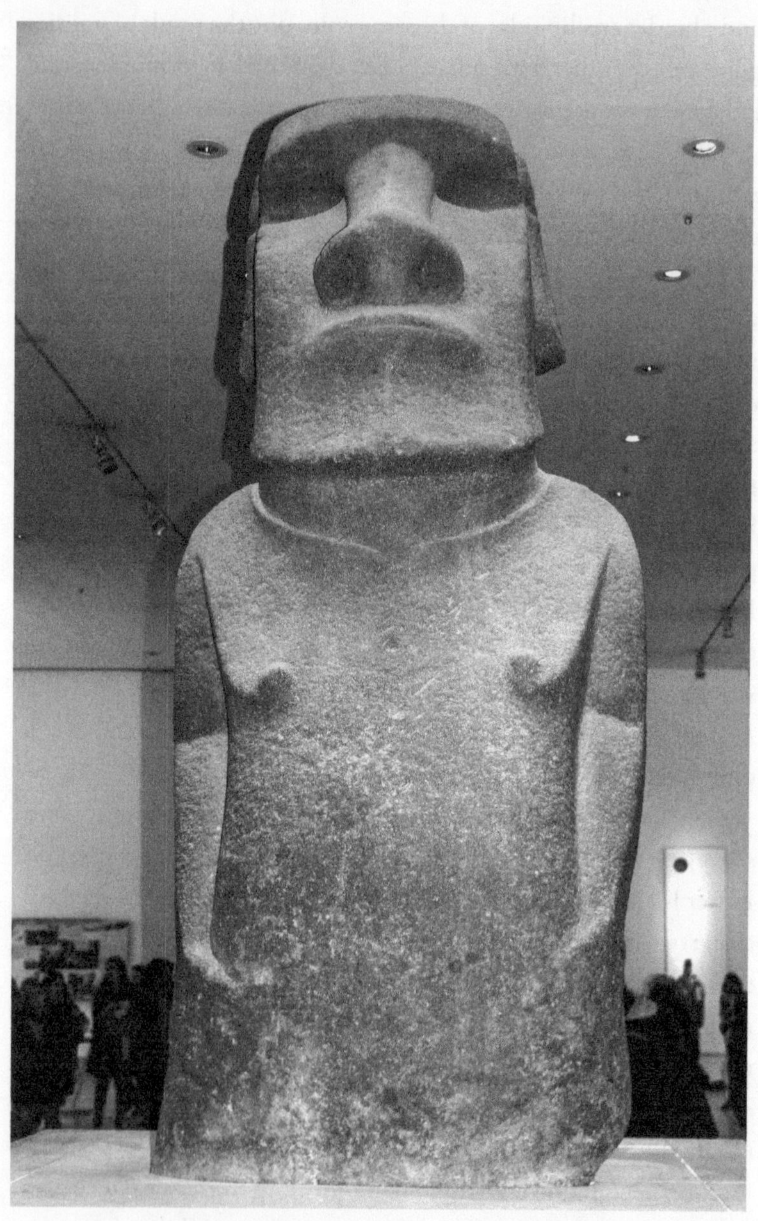

Hoa Hakananai'a at the British Museum, London.

out a political objective – scientific mapping, battlefield slaughter or organizing an exhibition for a museum in New York – and it was only in the act of fulfilling these primary directives that a secondary opportunity arose, on-the-fly so to speak, to acquire and disperse valuable works of art around the world.

The situation that greeted the crew of the *Topaze* on Easter Island was grim, to say the least. Though the islanders had always been one of the most isolated population groups in the world and had long been forced to grapple with the serious ecological disadvantages of their unique environment, the dual impact of Old World germs and guns constituted devastation on an entirely different scale. Once home to roughly 3,000 people, Easter Island was now nearly empty: just over one hundred people remained. They split their political loyalties among four different native chiefs, who in turn alternately cooperated and squabbled with a handful of Christian missionaries and a freebooting Frenchman named Jean-Baptiste Dutrou-Bornier. Over the previous decades, it had become abundantly clear that no indigenous Polynesian island or even an entire archipelago could stand alone against the encroachment of the outside world. A seismic shift in Pacific politics was underway. One by one every island kingdom had fallen under Western control or influence: the Society Islands, New Zealand, Hawaii, the Marquesas, the Tuamotus and Samoa.

This was the political backdrop to the arrival of HMS *Topaze* in November 1868. Few islanders – indigenous or Western – would have held any illusions about the future of Easter Island. If mighty Tahiti and Hawaii had been unable to keep the outside world at bay, what hope was there for tiny, impoverished Easter Island? It was in just such a geopolitical context that the British crew disembarked from their ship and began to explore the island. As was common in nearly all cross-cultural encounters in the Pacific over the previous century since Cook, the islanders were eager to trade for foreign goods. The captain of HMS *Topaze*, Commodore Richard Powell, lent carpenters, nails and planks to Dutrou-Bornier (who was attempting to build a schooner to sail to Tahiti) and distributed food and other provisions to the native community.

The islanders responded by offering in return what meagre resources they had: wooden crafts, song and dance performances, and – if a century of past precedent is any guide – sex. They also offered guides to escort the British crew around the island. On one of these forays, Lt Matthew Harrison noted that his native guides 'were much delighted with white trousers & shirts which we gave them'.[2] Over the next few days, indigenous guides led different parties of the crew to the two moai statues that would eventually be taken back to London. Though we lack any unmediated native perspectives on their removal, there are several eyewitness descriptions from the crew that are revealing. One participant in the transport of Hoa Hakananai'a across 5 kilometres (3 mi.) of rough terrain noted the availability of 'many willing hands', an apparent reference to the approximately sixty indigenous islanders who lent their assistance to the statue's removal. In addition, the islanders were said to have 'cheered' when the statue was floated out to the ship at anchor and successfully hoisted aboard. The event was so memorable that one islander named Tepano even had the scene tattooed on his arm, while another woman named Veriamu could still recall – decades later – the song sung by the English sailors as they transported the heavy megalith.[3] (The fact that the name 'Hoa Hakananai'a' literally means 'stolen' or 'hidden friend' in the local Polynesian dialect is unlikely to have constituted a moral judgement by islanders on the British removal, since the moai already bore this name when British officers were led to it – more likely this enigmatic name is a reference to an earlier unknown event in the statue's prehistory.)

However, perhaps the most telling piece of documentation was a handwritten letter given to Commodore Powell upon his departure from Easter Island. It was a petition from the ruling council – four native chiefs, Dutrou-Bornier and a Catholic missionary named Gaspar Zumbohm – to the French ambassador in Valparaíso requesting that France annex the island as a protectorate. France rejected it – not only this one, but four additional petitions submitted over the next two decades. These petitions provide useful context for the account of a French expedition in 1872 that found one attractive moai too heavy to load onto its ship. The solution was to saw its head off. Not only did the entire community witness this event, but they 'dramatically participated in it'.[4] Placed in its proper historical context, this 'desecration' is easy to understand. The moai, silent sentries who had stood watch over their clans for centuries, had failed to protect their descendants from near extinction in the modern world. As a result, these once sacred statues were not quite so sacred any more. Far better to turn them into silent diplomatic ambassadors that might encourage a powerful global empire to take Easter Island under its protective wing – a modern twist on a traditional symbol of native power.

In the end, it was Chile, not France, that annexed Easter Island in 1888. But this unexpected turn of political fate should not distract us from an obvious conclusion: Hoa Hakananai'a and Moai Hava were presented to the crew of HMS *Topaze* as diplomatic gifts. Their function was much the same as the replica moai presented by the Chilean ambassador to American University 132 years later: both of them represented an acknowledgement of friendly relations in the present and a tangible investment in the possibility of an even more fruitful political relationship in the future. In both cases, something of only modest value to the giver (spiritually diminished moai or a bulky replica) was exchanged for something of greater perceived value (political protection or favourable press on a major urban university campus). The exchange left both sides content, without any hint of acrimony or regret at the loss of whatever political or material favours had been tendered.

Another example of a diplomatic gift that originated in a remote Polynesian society is the magnificent feathered cloak from Hawaii known as an 'ahu'ula. Painstakingly woven from the bright yet delicate feathers of the now extinct mamo bird, each 'ahu'ula required tens of thousands of these birds to complete and were only worn by the Hawaiian nobility. Today, a casual visitor who encounters one of these cloaks in the British Museum may very well assume that such an artefact was 'stolen' by one means or another. But historical records leave little doubt about how it passed into British hands: the specimen held in the British Museum was given as a gift to Lt Charles Clerke, the captain of James Cook's sister ship on his third and final voyage into the Pacific. In 1778, when Cook and Clerke rediscovered the Hawaiian archipelago for the first time since the original Polynesian colonization more than half a millennium before, both sides of the encounter sought to enlist the other as a friendly ally that could prove useful in future endeavours. In an attempt to solidify just such a political bond, both Cook and Clerke were given the most valuable material gift that any Hawaiian tribe could produce at the time: an 'ahu'ula cloak comprised of hundreds of thousands of feathers from the mamo bird, to be worn only by a great chief and his lieutenants. Just as was the case with the moai from Easter Island, the fact that these political bonds did not bear the intended fruit – Cook was killed by Hawaiians just one year after receiving his cloak, while France did not annex Easter Island – is ultimately beside the point. For our purposes here, we need merely note that this is yet another classic case of a diplomatic gift, one that was tendered freely, knowingly and in exchange for immediate or anticipated political favours.

Some of the most famous diplomatic gifts have come not from remote islands in the Pacific but from the ruins of ancient civilizations that rose and fell along the shores of the Mediterranean. The notoriety of the Elgin Marbles – fragments of ancient Greek sculpture

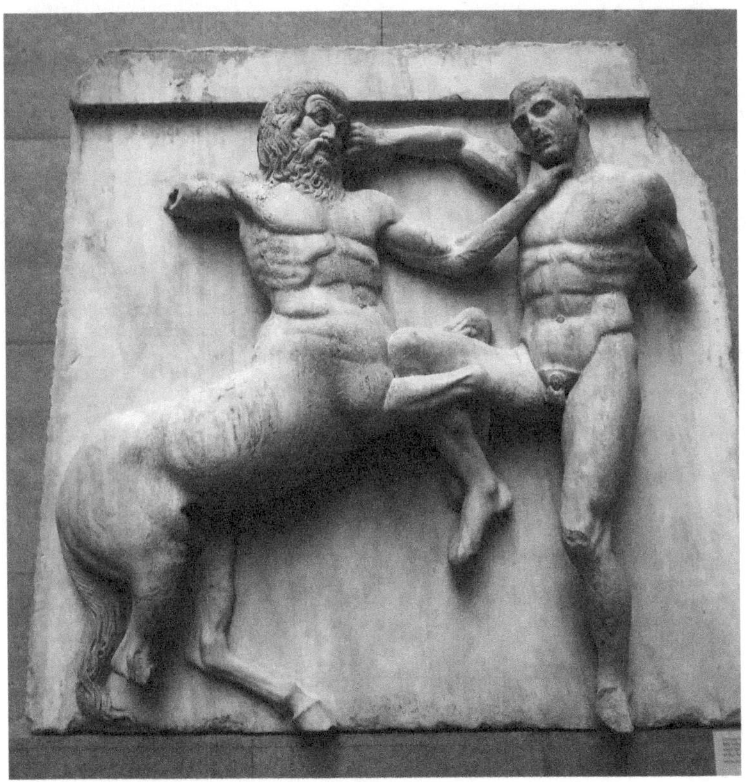

Centaur versus Lapith metope from the Parthenon at the British Museum, London.

that once adorned the elevated metopes, frieze and pediments of the Parthenon in Athens – is well known to all. Yet the heated debates about whether or not the sculptures should be returned to Greece all trace their origins back to new ideas that arose in the years *after* Elgin took them to England. When we examine the historical record concerning the actual course of events that led to their removal in Athens, it is clear that they represent yet another clear-cut case of a diplomatic gift freely tendered.

The key to understanding how the Elgin Marbles ended up in the British Museum lies in a proper understanding of just who Elgin was. Born to an ancient and distinguished family, Thomas Bruce inherited his earldom at just five years old. A successful career in the military led to an equally successful career in politics, first as a Scottish peer in the House of Lords and later as one of Britain's top diplomats in Vienna and Brussels. When Napoleon launched an invasion of the Ottoman province of Egypt in 1798 – motivated in part by a wish to cut off British access to India via the Mediterranean and Red Sea – London responded by dispatching its first permanent ambassador to Constantinople in order to cultivate a closer relationship with Selim III, the Ottoman sultan.

Lord Elgin, advised by his doctor to seek out warmer climes for his health, lobbied successfully for the post. He and his wife arrived in Constantinople in November 1799. To the sultan, the British represented the only realistic hope of getting Egypt back from the French. Thus Lord Elgin, as the chief diplomatic representative of Great Britain, became the primary conduit through which Ottoman gratitude for the British defeat of Napoleon in Egypt would be expressed. The sultan constantly showered Elgin with gifts that posterity has long forgotten about: snuff boxes, medals, horses, fur-lined cloaks, feathered headdresses and other expensive aristocratic baubles. The one gift that no one has ever forgotten about, however, is his firman.

A firman was a written authorization from the Ottoman government granting its bearer permission to carry out certain activities throughout the empire with the expectation of local assistance. Since Elgin, who fancied himself something of an intellectual and art aficionado, wanted to bring back samples of ancient Greek art for the avowed purpose of stimulating 'the progress of the Fine Arts in Great Britain', he applied for a firman that would allow him to do precisely that. But his original request bore little resemblance to the more than 100 tonnes of sculpture that he would eventually remove from the Ottoman province of Greece. In fact, Elgin had only requested authorization for his team of artisans in Athens to make plaster casts of the Parthenon sculptures – not to remove them. Selim III quickly approved the firman.

Now the story takes a fascinating turn. Faced with the arrival of Elgin's team of architects and artists in Athens, the local Ottoman governor turned them away at the base of the Acropolis, the rocky hill which overlooks the city amid a forest of ancient ruins, including the Parthenon. But the reason for their refusal had nothing to do with any notion that the Parthenon was a symbol of the Greek nation that should not be violated by foreigners. Instead, it was only because the Acropolis was then serving as a military citadel for the Ottoman army. That is, it was a strategic military site, with incomparable views of any incoming army or navy that might threaten the city. It was also densely packed with the military barracks and homes of Turkish soldiers and their families, along with a Muslim mosque that had been erected boldly right inside the ruined shell of the Parthenon.

It is important to stress that there was nothing illegitimate or inauthentic about this state of affairs. Our current fixation on the Elgin

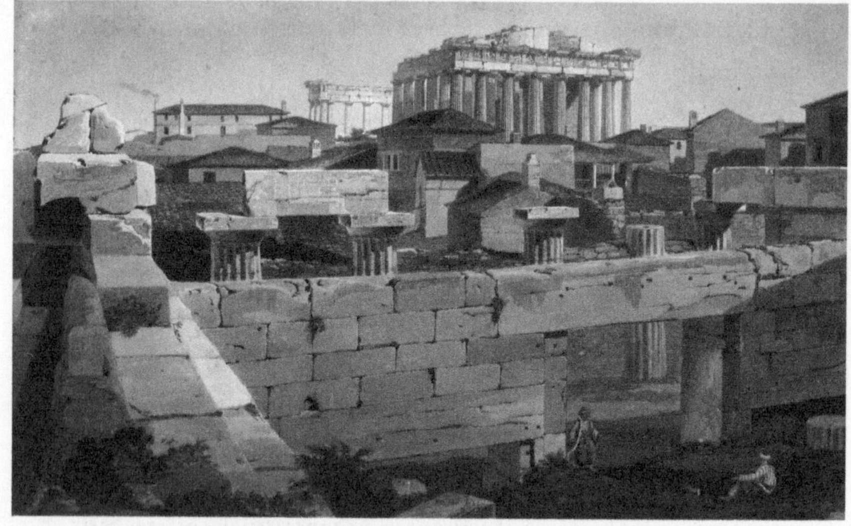

View of the Acropolis as a Turkish military garrison and residence, 1819, aquatint by Edward Dodwell.

Marbles as an enduring symbol of the supposedly eternal Greek nation is a modern distortion fostered by nationalist ideas that only arose in the decades after Elgin's ambassadorship. Throughout its more than 2,000 years of history, the Acropolis has been home to ancient Greek temples, Christian churches, brothels and Muslim mosques – often with the same building serving each function successively. The Parthenon was a Christian church for just as long as it was a pagan Greek temple, and it operated as a Muslim mosque for half that time again. There is no single 'rightful' identity that can be pulled out of this cultural melange. It was only in the 1820s and '30s, when European imperial powers decided to privilege the ancient Greek identity over all others as a means of encouraging Greek secession from the Ottoman empire, that the Parthenon came to assume its present symbolism as the quintessential symbol of authenticity for the modern Greek nation.

But the Athens of Lord Elgin's day was quite different. Back then, the majority of those people who would have identified as Greek professed the Eastern Orthodox Christian faith and would have been appalled at the idea that their ancestors, so to speak, had once sacrificed so many oxen in homage to Athena that rivers of blood had flowed by the Parthenon for hours on end. And if they could travel back in time, they would also find that communication was impossible: the Greek language evolved much in the way that Spanish, French and Italian had evolved out of Latin (and no one refers to the Romans as 'ancient Italians'). Athens itself was a small but cosmopolitan city, with Greek Christians accounting for only about half of its population. And there is no evidence to suggest that any of these Greeks viewed the Parthenon as an inviolable symbol of their 'nation': much like the Turkish soldiers in their midst, the Greek residents of Athens frequently quarried the ruins of the Acropolis as building materials for their own homes.

After he was denied access to the Acropolis by the local governor on the authority of his first firman, Elgin applied for a second one. He told the sultan all about the rude handling of his team in Athens. The sultan, incensed that some crumbling pagan marble might sour his relationship with the man who represented his best chance to recover Egypt from Napoleon, quickly issued a second firman and ordered a special envoy to deliver it in person to the local governor in Athens. Not only did the firman again authorize the taking of plaster casts, but it was accompanied by an oral threat from the sultan: if any more complaints reached his ears via Lord Elgin, the military governor's son would be sent as a slave to the galleys. These threats completely changed the balance of power in Athens. As Philip Hunt, a chaplain engaged by Elgin for his team in Athens, wrote, the local governor 'is now submissive to all our views in hopes of your speaking favourably for him' to the sultan.[5]

Sensing an opportunity, Hunt decided to reach for the stars: instead of plaster casts, might the sultan's favourite ambassador in Constantinople now be allowed to remove the original sculptures themselves? Aware that the sultan cared far more about the recovery of Egypt than a collection of ancient pagan sculptures that no one had tended for millennia, the governor agreed. But there is no reason to suppose that this was a secret operation, carried out under cover of dark, with objects spirited away as clandestine cargo in unmarked ships. A watercolour by Edward Dodwell, who witnessed at first hand the process of removal in 1801, shows local men hired by Elgin's team lowering a metope to the ground with rope under a cloudy but bright sky, as two well-dressed Turks (likely officials) sit on the ground nearby and smoke their pipes. The mosque, a symbol of a very different cultural orientation than we are used to associating with the Parthenon today, appears prominently inside the colonnade.

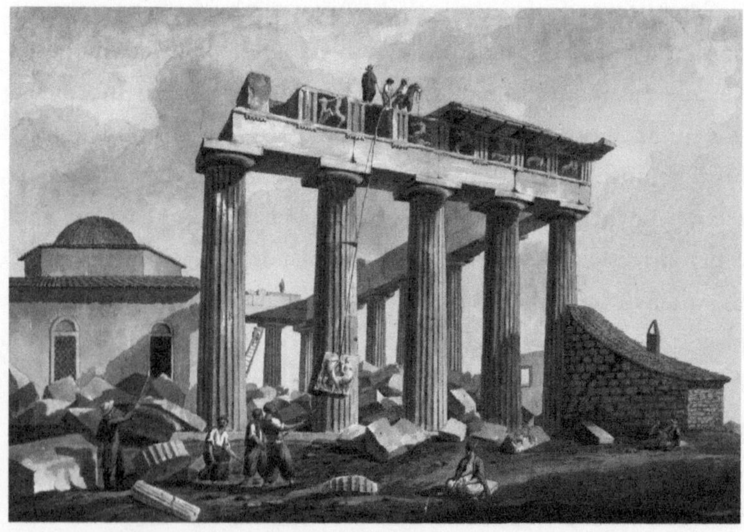

Lord Elgin's removal of the Parthenon sculptures, *c.* 1801–5, watercolour by Edward Dodwell.

In addition to being removed in broad daylight from the single most conspicuous and exposed site in all of Athens, these marbles also would have had to be laboriously transported to the nearest seaport, in full view of Ottoman officials and curious onlookers.[6]

To label the Elgin Marbles a form of military plunder is a gross perversion of historical fact. On the contrary, Elgin was the human embodiment of the exact opposite: his presence in Constantinople represented a military alliance between the British and Ottomans. And the sculptural programme he was permitted to remove from the Parthenon was a direct material extension of this alliance. Like many diplomatic gifts, such as was the case with Hoa Hakananai'a, the Elgin Marbles were not the result of a premeditated imperialist conspiracy. Permission to remove them arose from a serendipitous convergence of fluid developments on the ground while carrying out a very different political mission altogether. And both sides left the encounter in high spirits: Elgin got his marbles and the sultan got his Egyptian province back. Rarely has any diplomatic gift of art been so easy to identify as such.

Just as one famous diplomatic gift set sail for London, another only slightly less famous one soon followed in its wake. This is the 6.5-tonne exquisitely carved block of granite popularly known as the Memnon Head (the Younger Memnon). Later identified as an ancient Egyptian bust of the great pharaoh Ramesses II, it was one of the first specimens of pharaonic chiselwork to be regarded by Europeans as worthy of comparison to Greek and Roman fine art. It is now installed on top of an unadorned pedestal in the British Museum, visible from any corner of its spacious gallery. The story of its removal to England will once again lay bare all the hallmarks of diplomatic gifts: an unrelated political mission, serendipitous opportunity, unabashed labour in the light of day and zero regret.

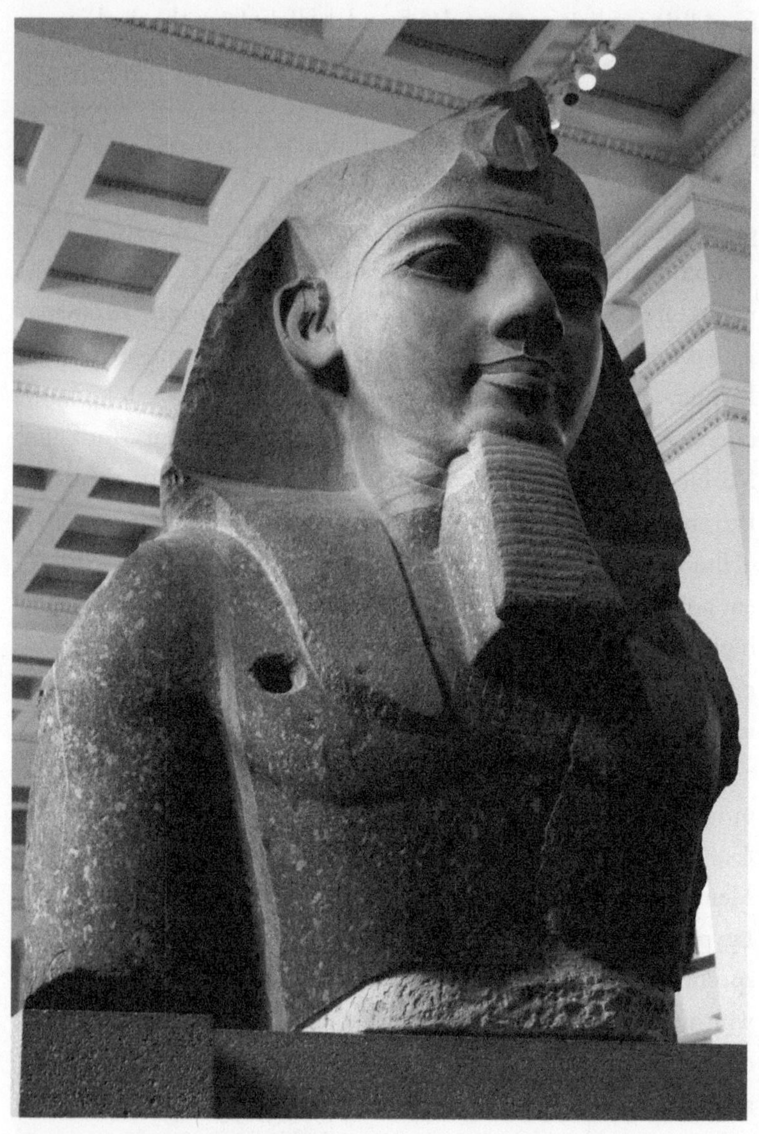

The Younger Memnon at the British Museum, London.

In 1801 the French, bombarded by the same British naval and land attack that prompted the sultan to indulge all of Lord Elgin's desires in Athens, began to withdraw from Egypt. The British army soon followed, leaving the fate of Egypt to be determined by a collection of loosely allied Ottoman combatants. Muhammad Ali, an Albanian military general drawn from the eastern Mediterranean cosmopolitan elite that had long made up much of the upper echelons of the Ottoman state, soon emerged victorious. Before long, he adopted the title of pasha and ruled Egypt as an Ottoman province in name but an independent fiefdom in practice. With political relations between Cairo and Constantinople often tense and adversarial, both the pasha and the sultan were eager to cultivate continued goodwill with both the French and British.

It was within this context that a man named Henry Salt arrived in Cairo in 1816 to take up the post of British consul. One of his first items of business was to apply for a firman from Muhammad Ali that would permit a team of excavators to remove ancient Egyptian antiquities at ancient sites along the Nile. Just as with Elgin in Constantinople, Salt had no trouble procuring such a firman, since the pasha wanted nothing more than to please London's man in Cairo as a means of cultivating powerful allies. If anything, Salt's application for a firman was looked upon by Muhammad Ali as merely an appetizer before the main course. Just one year before Salt arrived in Cairo as consul, the Swiss-English traveller John Lewis Burckhardt had tried to convince the pasha to deliver the Memnon Head to the prince regent in England as a present, but the pasha 'did not consider stone an appropriate gift'.[7]

Note that the pasha did not consider the Memnon Head to be a priceless symbol of the Egyptian nation. Quite the contrary: as a long-neglected hunk of pagan granite, it was perceived to be so bereft of any value that Muhammad Ali did not want to embarrass himself by presuming to give it away as a gift – even to someone who took great pains to suggest otherwise. The result was that the British would have to choose their own diplomatic gift. The man entrusted by Salt with the task of removing the Memnon Head was Giovanni Belzoni, a colourful figure whose chief qualification for the job appears to have been expertise in managing grand hydraulic spectacles in theatrical London productions, such as recreating a naval battle on stage. Belzoni, armed with Salt's firman, sailed to Luxor and hired a team of local peasants, or *fellahin,* to help him transport the Memnon Head nearly 5 kilometres (3 mi.) from its resting spot to the west bank of the Nile.[8]

There was nothing secretive about Belzoni's operations. En route to Luxor, he met the pasha's son, Ibrahim, whose staff checked his papers. By Ibrahim's side was the Italian collector Bernardino Drovetti, then serving as the French consul in Cairo. Much like Salt, Drovetti was leveraging the prospect of cosier relations with his homeland – in

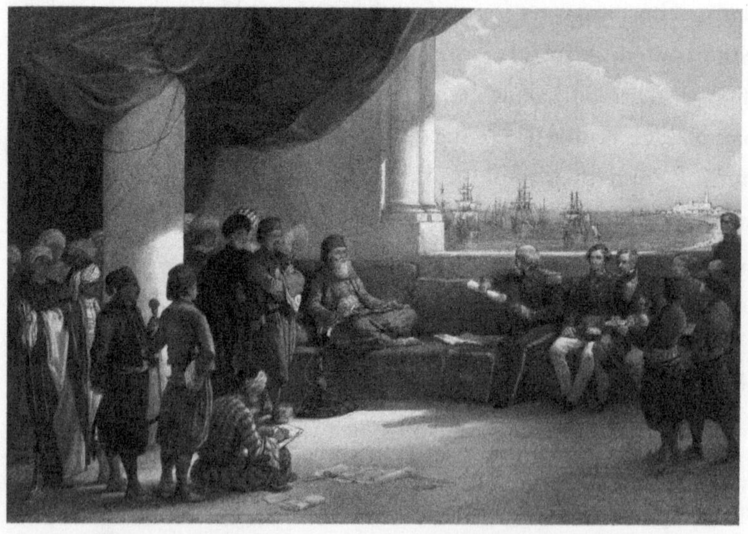

Egyptian pasha Muhammad Ali meeting with European diplomats, 1839, lithograph by Louis Haghe, 1848.

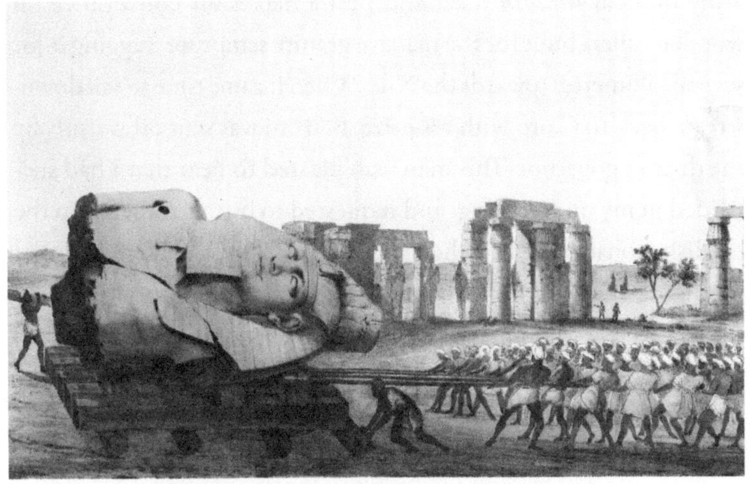

Belzoni's removal of the Young Memnon's Head, 1816, engraving by Agostino Aglio.

Drovetti's case, adopted homeland – to procure the right to remove ancient artefacts. To everyone they met throughout Egypt – be they Arabs, Albanians or Turks, high- or low-born – the terms offered were attractive. Ottoman diplomats found their political prospects brightened by association with the British or French, while Arab peasants procured an attractive supplemental income nearly always at or above market wages – and all for ancient works of heathen art whose only value had heretofore been calculated in terms of its economic value as building materials, as a substitute for manure (as crumbling remains were used as a substitute for fertilizer, as discussed later) or for the elusive gold often believed to be hidden inside.

In addition to both the pasha and his son being acutely aware of what Belzoni and Drovetti were doing, everyone in the vicinity of the Memnon Head clearly saw with their own eyes what was happening. In Belzoni's own memorable recollection of the removal, in which the Memnon Head appears far larger than its actual size, a veritable army of local *fellahin* push and pull a makeshift conveyance on wooden rollers built for the massive granite sculpture, tugging it for several kilometres towards the Nile. When it came time to sail downstream back to Cairo with his prize, Belzoni was sent off warmly by the district governor. This man was 'pleased to hear that I had succeeded in my undertaking, and requested to be remembered to the English Consul, to whom he had sent a letter by me'. Here again we see the local exchange of political favours, wherein the local governor expects to reap diplomatic rewards for his assistance in helping to organize a work team capable of removing a block of worthless granite. According to Belzoni, the district governor even attempted to refuse his money, in order 'to make a present' of the labour of his subjects. Belzoni refused, saying that Salt would not 'accept such a present'.[9]

What we see here, both in the case of Lord Elgin and Henry Salt, are various Ottoman officials, from the sultan in Constantinople to the pasha in Cairo to the district governor in Luxor, attempting to give the wrong type of gift to the British. So the British decided to take the initiative in pointing out what sort of gifts would actually be appreciated, much to the surprise of everyone they encountered. Still, since such foreign desires were so easy to satisfy, the local rulers repeatedly obliged. Once the Memnon Head arrived in Cairo on Belzoni's boat, it was even 'conveyed in safety to the Bashaw's magazine [that is, the pasha's warehouse], there to await its embarkation for England'.[10] And when Belzoni later returned to Cairo with the magnificent alabaster sarcophagus of the pharaoh Seti I – removed from the bowels of his tomb in the Valley of the Kings – Muhammad Ali even provided his personal ship to transport it the rest of the way to England. When William John Bankes, an English politician and budding Egyptologist, caught a glimpse of Seti's sarcophagus

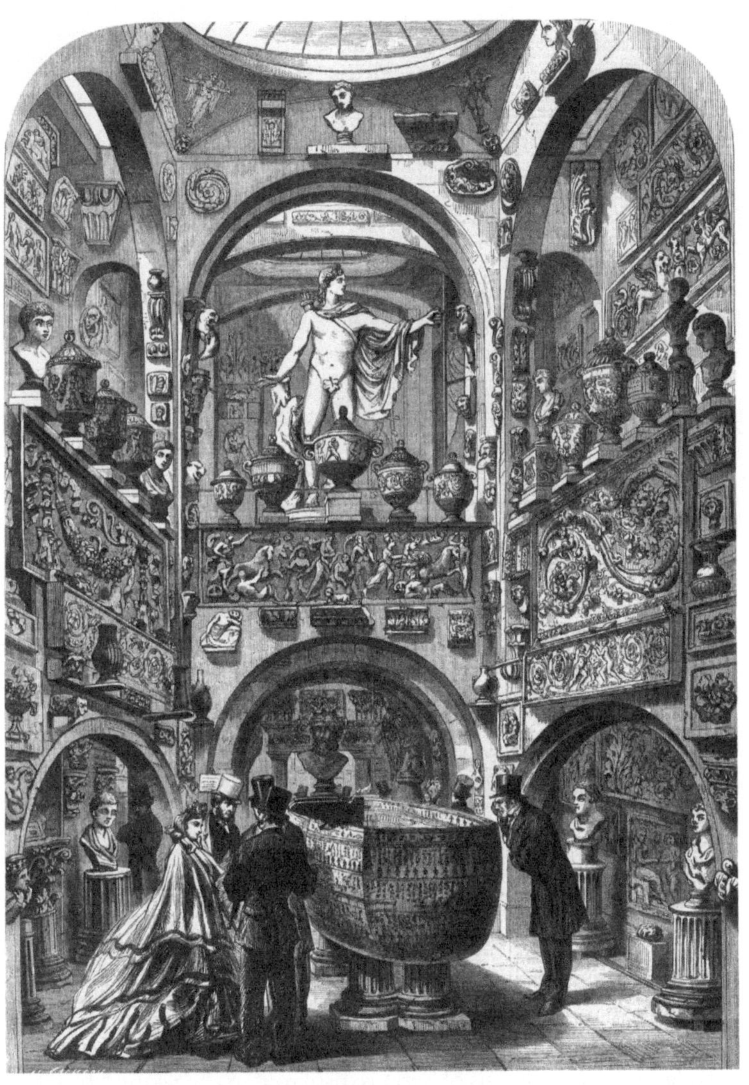

Sarcophagus of Seti I at Sir John Soane's Museum, London, engraving from *Illustrated London News*, 25 June 1864.

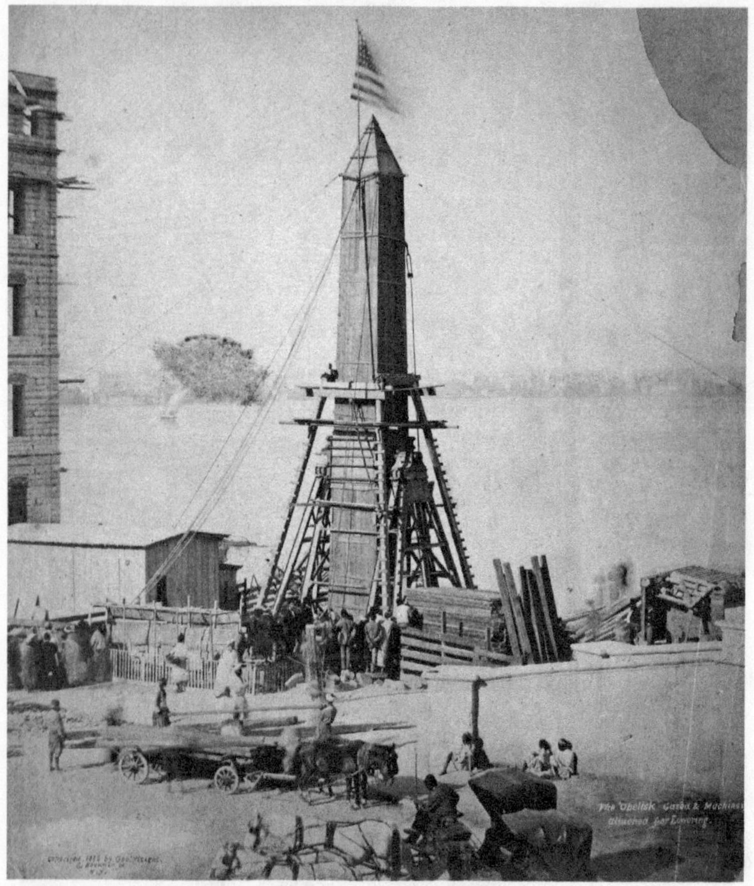

Cleopatra's Needle crated en route to New York's Central Park, 1880.

in London, he wrote that it 'had just arrived on a frigate belonging to the Pasha.'[11]

Today, the sarcophagus of Seti I is displayed in the Soane Museum in London. Museum-goers who cast their casual gaze over either splendid artefact – the bust of Ramesses II or the sarcophagus – may assume that they are stolen. But such an assumption couldn't be further from the historical truth. At every step of the way, Ottoman elites and Egyptian peasants knew exactly what Belzoni was doing on behalf of Henry Salt, and they had few qualms about lending their assistance to the cause, so long as they were provided with a form of compensation – wages, diplomatic favours – deemed more valuable than that which was taken away. Not only that, but they often explicitly referred to the assistance they exchanged in such endeavours as a present.

This practice of voluntarily gifting away the treasures of ancient Egypt to present or potential Western allies would continue for decades to come. In 1830 Muhammad Ali gifted to France one of the two ancient obelisks that once stood at the entrance to the Luxor Temple. It now stands in the Place de la Concorde. Not to be outdone, future pashas sent two additional obelisks from Alexandria to be erected in London and New York. They are popularly known as Cleopatra's Needles. At long last, the pasha and his descendants had finally come to terms with the fact that Westerners were not being disingenuous; that is, they really did want to assume the burden of transporting and preserving ancient pagan megaliths. To the Ottomans, such gifts were a no-brainer: something perceived as virtually worthless to them and their subjects could be magically transformed into hard-won political favours with hardly any effort on their part. And such practices have continued into our own modern era: in 1965 the Egyptian government disassembled and gifted an entire ancient edifice – the Temple of Dendur – to the Metropolitan Museum in New York as an expression of gratitude for American aid in helping to preserve other monuments threatened by the construction of the Aswan Dam.

Diplomatic gifts didn't always have to tip the scales in order to please their recipients. In fact, some of the most cherished antiquarian gifts in modern Chinese history have been among the smallest and most fragile. In 1907 the Qing dynasty official Duanfang, who travelled to the United States two years earlier to study modern conditions in Western countries, presented a Tang dynasty Daoist stele to the Field Museum in Chicago. The stele, which he described as an 'exceptionally fine and rare specimen of art', was presented to the museum 'as a souvenir' and 'a token of my pleasant remembrance of the trip'.[12] Even more famous than Duanfang's stele are the approximately 40,000 ancient manuscripts that were discovered in June 1900 by an itinerant Daoist priest in the secret cave library (now known as Cave 17) at the Mogao Grottoes near the oasis of Dunhuang. Comprised mostly of

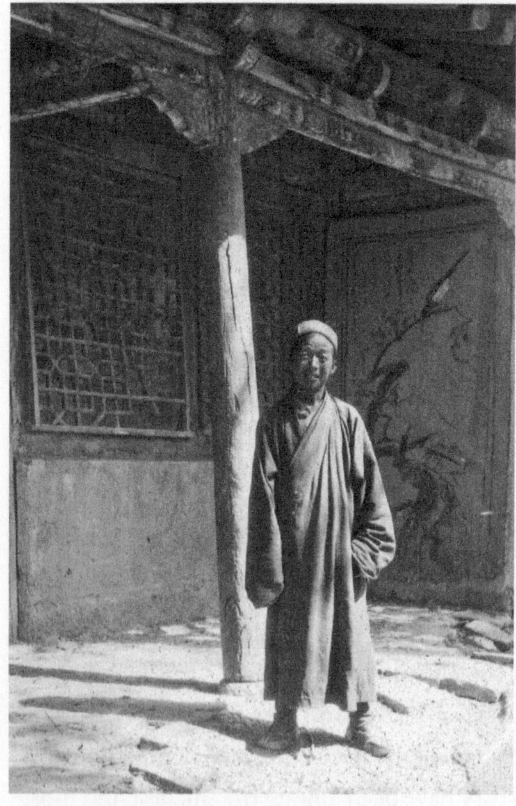

Wang Yuanlu, caretaker of Cave 17, 1907, photograph by Aurel Stein.

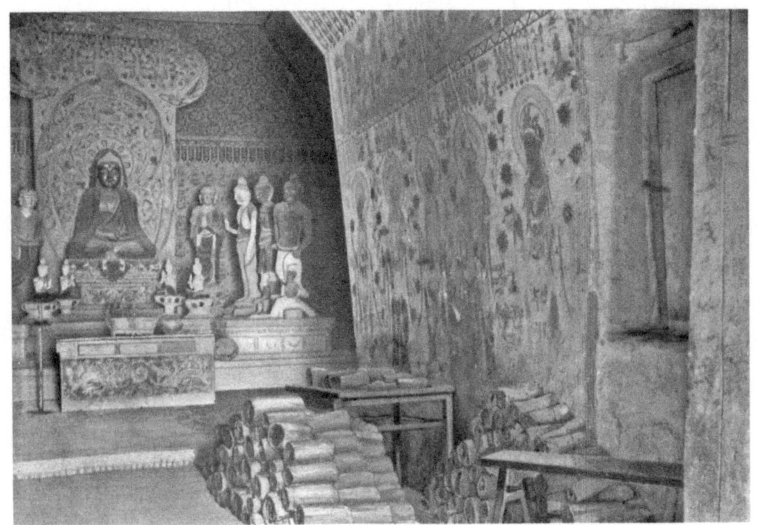

Ancient scrolls piled up alongside the entrance to Cave 17 (drawn on the negative of the image).

Buddhist sutras written in Chinese and Tibetan during the second half of the first millennium AD, these immaculately preserved scrolls came to light a full seven years before the first Westerner – the Hungarian-born British archaeologist Aurel Stein – managed to visit the cave. As such, they provide a wonderful case study of how Chinese people of all social classes interacted with newly unearthed antiquities before, during and after the arrival of Western collectors.

The secret cave library at Dunhuang was discovered by the illiterate Daoist priest Wang Yuanlu after he decided to widen a crack in the plaster on a wall to see if anything lay on the other side. He was rewarded for his efforts with not only the revelation of those 40,000 ancient manuscripts but an Aladdin's cave of mostly religious artwork and other small treasures. But what interests us most today is what he decided to do with them. Unable to read any of the scrolls himself, Wang decided to send selected batches of the most exquisitely produced specimens to various Chinese government officials in nearby towns as gifts. His hope was that they would reciprocate by sending him a cash donation for the restoration of the fast-deteriorating temple and caves at the Mogao Grottoes.

In this hope he was severely disappointed. Nevertheless, this marked the earliest dispersal of these precious antiquities into the outside world. Unlike nearly all the other diplomatic gifts we have examined so far, the Dunhuang manuscripts were not simply lying idle under the sun, mostly ignored by the throngs of people who saw them on a daily basis. They had to be discovered, and that discoverer had a name. This brings us to an important question: did anyone at the time believe that these manuscripts were a symbol of the Chinese nation and thus belonged to that nation? When Stein met Wang for the first time seven years later and was permitted a brief glimpse at the secret cave library, he recorded his own snap judgement in his diary. Wang, he said, was the 'undisputed owner of collection by right of discovery'.[13] Wang's decision to send a handful of scrolls to nearby Chinese officials as gifts and then sell successive batches to both Stein and later Western visitors seems to suggest that he agreed with Stein's assessment.

But what about the Chinese officials to whom Wang sent his early gifts? In 1910 Wang Shu'nan, the Xinjiang minister of finance, observed that a great many previously unknown antiquities had recently emerged from the desert sands of the northwestern regions and been taken away by Westerners. 'But the earth does not love its treasures,' Wang wrote. 'Henceforth, who knows how many more will emerge from the ground?'[14] A very similar sentiment was expressed by another Chinese antiquarian concerning the sudden appearance of Shang dynasty oracle bones in the agricultural heartland at about the same time. In 1903 he wrote that the oracle bones had been 'long buried, yet suddenly exposed by the opening of a new footpath. The earth does not love its treasures. Once struck by the light of day, they supply lovers of antiquity and connoisseurs of the marvelous.'[15]

Today, the dispersal of the treasures of the secret cave library at Dunhuang is widely regarded within China as an immoral act of imperialist theft and domestic corruption. A century ago, however, a very different ethos prevailed, one familiar to any school playground: finders keepers. No one could claim prior ownership over something that the earth itself had kept buried for hundreds or even thousands of years. As a result, Wang was free to either sell or give away the manuscripts he himself had discovered. And crucially, it wasn't just Stein and Wang who believed in the right of discovery and sanctity of private ownership. Educated and privileged Chinese elites also subscribed to this position. The subsequent actions of those who received Wang's early gifts makes this abundantly clear.

First, none of the Chinese officials to whom Wang gifted a scroll made any attempt to donate it to an imperial institution (such as a library or academy) or to try to force Wang to do the same. Instead, they treated these gifts as legitimate perks of their elevated station in life, and then proceeded to treat them exactly as Wang had treated them: as gifts to other people in higher positions of authority than themselves. We might say that this is the essence of a diplomatic gift, be it within the context of an asymmetrical power relationship between British and Ottoman officials, an illiterate Daoist priest and educated Chinese officials, lower-ranking Chinese officials and higher-ranking Chinese officials, or Chinese officials and Western officials. In this sense, the Chinese engagement with the Dunhuang manuscripts provides us with the most complete case study of all. This is because, unlike the Turks and Egyptians, educated Confucian gentleman did in fact continue to value the cultural productions of all earlier eras in the history of Chinese civilization, from oracle bones that recorded human sacrifice in 1250 BC to Buddhist sutras from the Tang dynasty (AD 618–907).

Despite this unique perception of cultural continuity among the Chinese, the end result was largely the same. Just because they valued the Dunhuang manuscripts more than Egyptian elites valued the Memnon Head does not mean that these educated Chinese officials believed they belonged to the Chinese themselves or a 'Chinese nation'. It merely increased the value of political favours that they expected to receive in return from whomsoever they chose to target for its subsequent regifting. And this person could be either Chinese or Western – the only precondition was that the recipient appreciate the value of the gift and feel inclined to reciprocate in some way. In 1908 the French scholar Paul Pelliot, hot on the heels of Stein, also passed through the northwestern desert regions of the Qing empire. When Pelliot paid a visit to the Manchu prince Zailan in the provincial capital of Ürümchi, his host gave him a 1,300-year-old manuscript from Dunhuang as a gift. Once he arrived at the town of Dunhuang itself, the local prefect gave him two additional ancient manuscripts from the secret cave library, to which, according to Pelliot's diary, 'he does not attach a price'.[16]

No single scroll from Cave 17 better illustrates these themes, however, than a Tang dynasty copy of the *Sutra on the Solemn Attainment of Buddhahood*, which was one of the first scrolls that Wang chose to send as a gift to Chinese officials. Ping Foong, a curator at the Seattle Art Museum, has completed a painstaking reconstruction of the scroll's labyrinthine path through numerous social networks once it left Wang's hands.[17] The first lucky recipient was Yan Dong, a high-ranking Qing official stationed near Dunhuang, in either late 1900 or early 1901. Within mere months of receiving this unexpected treasure, however, Yan decided to regift it to Paul Splingaerd, a foreigner then serving in the employ of the Qing government who was popularly known at the time as 'the Belgian Mandarin'. Splingaerd didn't hold on to the scroll for long either, regifting it yet again to its most eminent owner yet: Rao Yingqi, governor of the neighbouring province of Xinjiang.

Having sat idle in a moisture-less cave for nine hundred years, this *Sutra on the Solemn Attainment of Buddhahood* was now travelling at comparative light speed. In 1903 Governor Rao died in the oasis of Hami and the scroll passed into the hands of his family. Rao's wife then took both the sutra and the remainder of her family back to their hometown in Hubei – 2,400 kilometres (1,500 mi.) to the southeast. Then Rao Fenghuang, the governor's son, apparently confident in his right to inherit what nearly everyone in his day and age would have considered his family's private property, appears to have cut the sutra up into many different pieces over the next several decades in order to squeeze the greatest number of regifting opportunities out of the manuscript as possible. One of these fragments ended up in the hands of his daughter, Rao Yu'ai. In 1932 Yu'ai regifted her fragment of the sutra to Anna Matilda Bille, her American teacher at Tsinghua University in Beijing, which shows once again that even as late as the 1930s highly educated Chinese – a category that now included women – felt that it was perfectly appropriate to give away China's national heritage (as we might characterize it today) to foreigners.

Having now logged close to 4,800 kilometres (3,000 mi.) over three decades, the Dunhuang sutra was apparently still filled with wanderlust. In 1933 Bille retired from teaching and took the sutra fragment with her to Honolulu, where it lay inside 'a trunk with moth balls and at ambient temperatures and humidity'. When Bille in turn died in 1942 – the second owner to pass away with the manuscript still in his or her possession – she bequeathed it to her former Chinese student Fook-tan Ching. Ching then gave it to his own son, who finally donated it to the Seattle Art Museum soon after he learned about a 2016 exhibition on the caves of Dunhuang.

Is this well-travelled sutra an emblem of imperialist plunder? Hardly. On the contrary, it illustrates perhaps better than any other example just how differently our ancestors – be they Turkish, Egyptian, Greek, European, American or Chinese – interacted with the material remains of ancient civilizations. Though these objects may now be considered to be inviolable symbols of our respective national essences, they were clearly not regarded as such just a few generations ago. The gifting and regifting of art and antiquities has one of the longest pedigrees in history. This long-standing practice made it possible for people in more humble positions of authority – or in the case of a student gift to a teacher, no authority at all – to cultivate a more productive relationship with someone in a superior position of authority for the mutual benefit of all concerned. Diplomatic gifts were ideal for situations in which the exchange of money would be regarded as impractical or useless (Easter Island), as a sign of corruption (local officials in Athens and Luxor), or as a sign of uncouth behaviour unworthy of a gentleman or a lady (Chinese officials and American teachers). As the gifting behaviour of Belgian official Paul Splingaerd demonstrates – he both received and regifted the Dunhuang sutra – it did not matter if the giver belonged to the same race or nation as the recipient. What mattered was that the antiquity being exchanged was perceived as an acknowledgement of the actual or anticipated relationship between giver and recipient.

Taken as a whole, the number of diplomatic gifts in Western museums is probably not very large when contrasted with the size of any given collection in its entirety. But since they tended to be collected by educated people who knew what they wanted and had enough resources to manage their removal, transportation and preservation over a period of many years, these types of antiquities tend to be visually spectacular and historically significant, with a public profile that few other objects can match. Hoa Hakananai'a, the Elgin Marbles and the Memnon Head constitute just a handful of the 8 million objects held at the British Museum, but they garner a disproportionate amount of popular and scholarly attention. There are only two ancient Egyptian obelisks in London and New York, but they are seen by millions of commuters and tourists every year. The casual observer, inundated with unsubstantiated claims of imperialist theft and plunder, may very well assume that these are all stolen. But history tells us otherwise.

Nevertheless, it most certainly does not follow that just because two or three ancient Egyptian obelisks left Egypt as diplomatic gifts, every single Egyptian obelisk ever to have left Egypt also did so as a type of diplomatic gift. This is emphatically not the case. In fact, of the approximately thirty ancient Egyptian obelisks still intact today, fewer than one-third remain standing in Egypt. The city of Rome alone has eight of them – and perhaps as many as 48 in antiquity – all taken as symbols of Roman military conquests in Egypt in the centuries following the downfall of Antony and Cleopatra. Among their number is the tallest standing obelisk in the world, towering just over 32 metres (105 ft) in front of the Lateran Basilica.[18]

So the majority of ancient Egyptian obelisks erected in Western metropolises were indeed the products of military plunder – but not modern plunder. As we have seen, the three obelisks sent to London, Paris and New York over the course of the nineteenth century were voluntarily given away as diplomatic gifts. Such shades of nuance confuse not only present-day Western commentators, but Egyptian ones as well. In 2020 the Egyptian government's plan to install a newly unearthed obelisk in the centre of Tahrir Square in Cairo elicited condemnation from domestic archaeologists. Monica Hanna, dean of the Arab Academy for Science, Technology and Maritime Transport, organized an online petition to oppose the move. 'Decorating western capitals with ancient Egyptian obelisks was a symbol of colonialism, a symbol of the West's power,' she said. 'Are we going to replicate that?'[19]

Hanna's criticism is only partially correct. Some obelisks, such as those in Rome, are indeed symbols of foreign imperialism, but it is an imperialism that ran its course well over a thousand years ago, long before our modern national identities emerged. And the terms of their removal were quite distinct from those three nineteenth-century obelisks that ended up in London, Paris and New York. The latter stemmed from the efforts of Egyptian politicians searching for an easy way to sweeten diplomatic negotiations by giving away something of little value to themselves but of great value to the recipient. (The fact that it took 1,900 years after the first obelisk was spirited away from Egypt by foreigners before a domestic Egyptian politician saw fit to erect a single obelisk in his own capital – despite ample supply at hand – underscores just how little valued they were in their own homeland.)

All of the ancient obelisks removed from Egypt before the nineteenth century, however, constitute clear-cut cases of military plunder. But the differences between these two categories are not apparent on a superficial glance: we cannot simply assume that any non-European antiquity on display in a European city was obtained through immoral means. There is a world of difference between the genteel parlour negotiations of unarmed diplomats and the bloody smash-and-grab actions of a menacing soldier in the heated fog of war. Military plunder was the only means of acquisition in which antiquities were removed at gunpoint without the consent of native owners or other nearby residents.

One rule of thumb is to look for visual evidence of uniformed soldiers and firearms in the documentation produced by the participants themselves. Paintings of the 1798 French invasion of Egypt depict Napoleon examining an upright mummy in a sarcophagus as uniformed soldiers equipped with rifles and bayonets look on. British

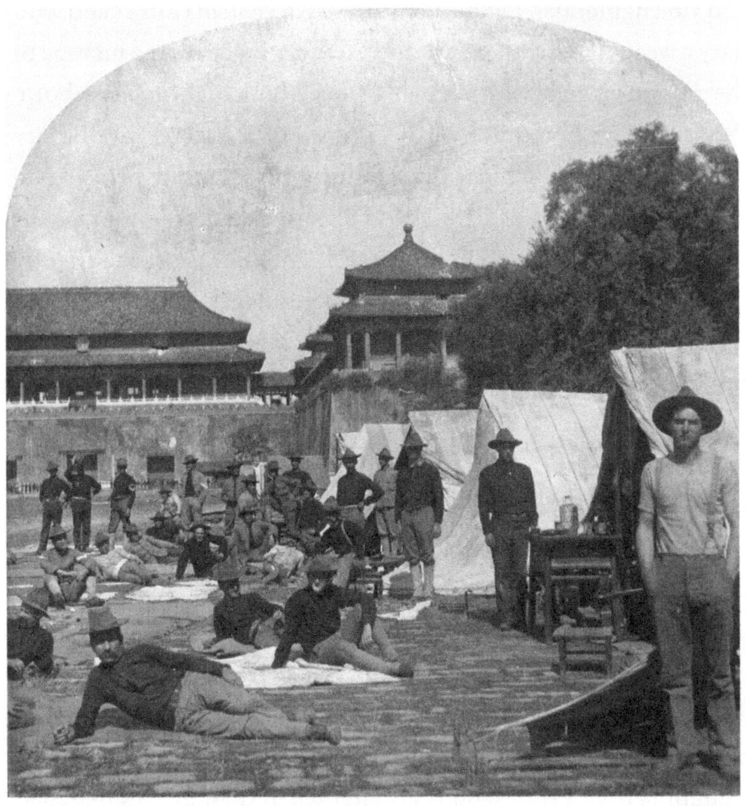

American soldiers in the Forbidden City courtyard, *c.* 1900.

soldiers who shot their way into the royal palace in the Benin Kingdom in February 1897 posed in uniform while sitting on a floor littered with looted ivory and bronzes. And uniformed members of the 9th U.S. Infantry posed for a photograph in the Forbidden City in August 1900 at the same time as looting of the imperial palace was under way.

Even a superficial glance at their visual counterparts for the Elgin Marbles, Memnon Head or Dunhuang manuscripts, however, are enough to highlight the dramatic differences between peaceful gifts and violent plunder. Elgin's men, dressed in civilian clothes and with nary a weapon in sight, slowly and excruciatingly lower a metope to the ground via rope with the help of locals both high- and low-born. Paul Pelliot's photograph of the interior of the secret cave library depicts an eclectic scholar draped in corduroy calmly perusing an ancient scroll by candlelight. And Howard Carter's photographs of the tomb of Tutankhamun show a well-groomed gentleman gently probing one of the pharaoh's inner sarcophagi with the aid of an Egyptian assistant – the only thing even remotely threatening about this bookish Egyptologist is the wooden cane he occasionally leaned on for support.

There is nothing new about military plunder. In fact, the coercive removal of art, antiquities and other cultural monuments on the backs of heavily armed soldiers appears to be about as old as history itself. Perhaps the earliest instance of documented military plunder concerns the fate of the victory stele of the Akkadian ruler Naram-Sin. Created around 2250 BC to commemorate the Akkadian conquest of the Lullubi people in a mountainous region of modern Iraq, it was plundered by a descendant of those same Lullubi people a thousand years later when their armies marched in the opposite direction.[20] After that, the annals of history are filled with accounts of temples ransacked and palaces burned to the ground – Persepolis, the Temple of Solomon, the Acropolis – but few details survive regarding what (if any) loot was taken away by the victorious armies.

The oldest and most detailed accounts of military plunder concern the Roman era. During their victory procession to celebrate the subjugation of the Greeks of Ambracia in 189 BC, the Roman army paraded 785 captured bronzes and 230 marble statues through Rome.[21] Over the next several centuries, as the empire expanded, plundered art from throughout the Mediterranean shores and beyond filled the streets and villas of Rome. The Roman historian Livy did not question the moral basis of such acquisitions. In reflecting on loot obtained from the sack of Syracuse, Livy concluded that it was 'no doubt the spoils of the enemy' and 'no doubt taken by right of war'. He was merely echoing the opinions of Greek philosophers before him: in the fourth century BC, Xenophon took it as a matter of course that victorious armies would claim the possessions of the vanquished. 'For who does not know that victors save their own possessions and take in addition what belongs to the defeated?'[22]

During Roman times, the only moral misgivings that surrounded the acquisition of military plunder concerned potential consequences for its new owners, not sympathy for its prior owners. One concern was that the craze for acquiring too much beautiful art could lead to moral degeneracy. But the much greater concern was that any loot taken from a religious site would incur a desire for revenge in the gods once associated with it. Such fears of spiritual retribution inspired many popular stories of vengeful gods wreaking havoc in the land of the conquerors. In response, plundered statues or other portable symbols of rival deities were sometimes brought to Rome in the midst of an elaborate ceremony designed to placate the migrating god. Referred to as *evocàtio*, these rituals were conceived as a sort of invitation for the god to abandon their ruined homeland and relocate to Rome.[23] During the Crusades, marauding Christians freshly returned from the sack of Constantinople created similar stories of migration, known as *translatio*, for the relics of saints that they had stolen from churches in the east. No one, it seems, lost much sleep over any prior attachments that the former owners of such relics may have had – they simply wanted to ensure that the supernatural wrath of the gods did not fall on their own heads as their earthly idols were kidnapped and spirited away to far-off lands.

Another perspective on the moral stakes of ancient military plunder can be found in discussions between generals and emperors in Chinese history regarding proper battlefield behaviour. In the year AD 630, a Tang general named Li Jing ambushed an Eastern Turk camp and routed its army. When his men took 'rare treasures' that once belonged to the khagan and his chiefs for themselves, the Tang emperor censured Li for not having these treasures sent directly to the emperor. Ten years later, another general likewise incurred the emperor's wrath when he 'wantonly seized rare curios for himself' from the conquered Central Asian outpost of Gaochang. In neither case did the emperor's anger derive from any sympathy he may have held for his looted foes on the battlefield. The only issue worthy of note at the time was that his soldiers and officers had selfishly kept the loot for themselves rather than first sending it to the emperor in the capital.[24]

Plunder could go both ways, however, and more often than not, it was the Chinese who were plundered by northern nomads from the Mongolian steppe rather than the other way around. By far the most famous instance of military plunder in Chinese history is the sack of Kaifeng, the capital of the Northern Song dynasty, by the nomadic Jurchen peoples in AD 1127. Huizong, the reigning Song emperor, was renowned for his unprecedented collection of Chinese art and antiquities: his catalogues of paintings and specimens of calligraphy alone list 7,617 items, in addition to 6,705 books and 840 antiquities. All of these treasures were dispersed across China when the city fell to the Jurchens and the emperor was taken captive. The fate of Huizong was treated as a cautionary tale in later dynasties: any monarch who 'let his interests in the arts go too far' would be reminded of the cruel fate that befell the last ruler to be overly distracted by cultural pursuits.[25]

These later Chinese critics attributed to Huizong a form of individual moral degeneracy not unlike Roman critiques of excessive collecting on the part of their own senators and generals. There was also a Chinese counterpart to the Roman fear of spiritual vengeance regarding kidnapped rival deities. During the Tang dynasty, it was standard practice for a conquering general to 'let the troops loose' (*zongbing*) upon victory. The only effective restraint on such behaviour was the strategic concern, only occasionally expressed by generals and emperors, that wanton rape, pillage and massacres would embolden future enemies to resist to the death – for who would ever surrender if they knew what sort of awful fate awaited them?[26] Here, instead of embittered gods, we see warnings of embittered subjects. But the Chinese could play the religion card as well. In 1411 the Ming eunuch-admiral Zheng He sailed his famous treasure fleet to the Indian Ocean and paid a visit to Sri Lanka. When an ill-advised attempt at what one historian has described as 'regime change' went awry, Zheng's army took the local Tamil king captive and made off with a sacred religious relic: one of the Buddha's teeth. The official justification for this brazen act of plunder, so similar to the actions of Christian crusaders in Constantinople, was that the Sri Lankan king had 'neglected' and 'insulted' Buddhism – thus making him unfit to serve as a steward of the holy relic any longer.[27]

These examples make it clear that, in the realm of art and antiquities, military plunder has an ancient pedigree equal to or even exceeding that of diplomatic gifts. Both practices were widespread across the globe and neither one elicited much moral handwringing from those who carried them out. In particular, military plunder has long been regarded as the rightful prerogative of any victorious army. When it was discussed at all, it was critiqued for reasons that sound quite strange to our ears today, such as its tendency to engender the wrath of vengeful gods or resentful subjects. More often than not, though, it wasn't criticized at all. The plunder of religious relics, be it in Constantinople or Sri Lanka, was routinely justified by claiming that the interests of the deity embodied by such relics would be better served alongside a new, more enlightened steward in a new land. Nowhere do we find a critique suggesting that the collective memories and stories of a nation were being wrongfully stolen by another nation. The only person who felt that his cultural treasures were being stolen from him was the Chinese emperor who chastised his generals in the field for denying him his rightful share – 100 per cent – of what was regarded at the time as legitimately plundered loot.

So neither military plunder nor critiques of military plunder are novel phenomena unique to our own day and age. But the content of such critiques did change significantly over the course of the late eighteenth and nineteenth centuries. One of the hallmarks of the new Age of Enlightenment was a belief that scientific methods of knowledge production would lead to a steady improvement in the condition of humankind. History now marched forward in steady progress towards a more humane and brighter future, and anyone not participating in this march would serve as a reminder of just how far enlightened Europeans had come. There were many ways for people during the Enlightenment to measure such progress, but the one most germane to our purposes here was the incessant comparison of supposedly 'civilized' and 'savage' peoples. And any time that 'civilized' peoples engaged in behaviours that were normally attributed only to 'savage' peoples – fairly or not – the self-appointed guardians of a newly enlightened moral standard were quick to pounce.

The rise of Napoleon on the European stage provided one of the first opportunities for the performance of this Enlightenment critique in the realm of art and antiquities. As French armies spilled out of France, their confiscation of numerous European art collections elicited widespread condemnation from rival political elites. In 1802 Lord Elgin wrote a letter in which he touted the virtues of his marbles and compared them to French military plunder in Europe, where 'Bonaparte has not got such a thing from all his thefts in Italy.'[28] It wasn't that Napoleon had neglected to provide a suitably enlightened cover story for these coerced seizures. After all, most of them were funnelled into galleries in the newly established Louvre – a veritable stone-and-mortar embodiment of Enlightenment ideals.

But few European elites were convinced by Napoleon's rhetorical gambit. In order for the new Enlightenment critique to sound plausible, the two poles of comparison – taker versus owner, civilized versus savage – must be separated by a certain degree of ethnic, cultural and economic distance. But in Europe, Napoleon plundered art that had previously belonged to people who were cut from the same cultural, economic and political cloth as himself. So sending this art to the Louvre fooled nobody. The new discourse was much more convincing, however, when applied to French military adventures in Egypt. In 1798, during his invasion of Egypt, Napoleon not only delivered on his promise to send many of the antiquities his

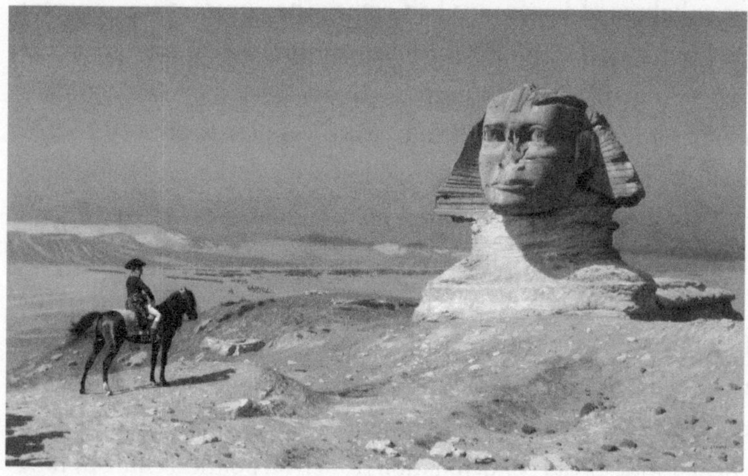

Napoleon before the Sphinx, oil on canvas painting by Jean-Léon Gérôme, 1886.

soldiers stumbled upon to the Louvre for scholarly study and preservation, but he took the unprecedented step of bringing along a team of 170 scholars from the Commission des sciences et des arts to interpret everything they found according to the latest scientific standards of the day.[29]

To observers back home, this was a much more convincing display of Enlightenment ideals. In Europe, Napoleon had behaved in a way that most of his European rivals regarded as barbarous, but in poor benighted Egypt the same gestures were regarded as a civilized exercise of scholarship worthy of commendation. At home, Napoleon was a brute by European standards, but outside Europe the standards were so low that the same sort of actions that would merit the label of military plunder back home were regarded in a much more positive light, and indeed were regarded as worthy of emulation by other European imperial powers.

In the final analysis, what we see with Napoleon's invasion of Egypt is the rise of a new rhetorical standard for when and where military plunder should be called out for what it really is: the coercive removal of cultural treasures behind the barrel of a gun. Now military plunder would only be labelled as such when it was carried out in a manner that made the 'civilized' aggressors of Europe resemble the 'savage' rivals from whom they were plundering. Bringing along a group of scholars and transferring loot to museums was what civilized people did. An orgy of disorganized looting by armed riff-raff hacking its way through enemy lines in search of a quick profit was what barbarous people did. No longer did Europeans worry about angering the kidnapped gods of foreign lands. Now they need only worry about whether or not they could legitimize the fruits of military plunder by associating it with museums and scholarly analysis. Whereas Zheng He once tried to justify his plunder of the Buddha's tooth from the Tamil king of Sri Lanka by claiming that the Chinese emperor would be a better spiritual patron for such a sacred relic, after 1798 French generals began to justify their seizure of Egyptian antiquities by claiming that Napoleon was a better scholarly patron of such objects.

From this point forward, Western military plunder outside Europe would be judged according to the new standards set down during Napoleon's invasion of Egypt. In October 1860 British and French soldiers looted the Old Summer Palace (Yuanmingyuan) on the outskirts of Beijing while engaged in military operations during the Second Opium War. Shortly thereafter, upon learning of the execution of several British prisoners who had been captured by the Chinese under a flag of truce, Lord Elgin – incredibly, the son of the same Lord Elgin who had removed the Parthenon marbles six decades earlier – ordered his troops to set fire to the entire summer palace complex. According to Lieutenant-Colonel Garnet Wolseley, the smoke was so thick that 'it seemed as if the sun was undergoing a lengthened eclipse.' A Chinese observer described 'a vast column of smoke [that] arose from the northwest direction ascertaining that the Barbarians had burnt the Summer Palace'.[30]

Though many hawkish proponents of imperialist wars back home were quick to defend Elgin's actions, other voices were more inclined to agree with the Chinese conclusion that such actions could only come from the hands of a barbarian. The first sign of anticipated moral guilt by the British and French participants in this act of military plunder came in the form of accusations that only one side or the other – that is, British or French soldiers – had actually participated in the looting. One British account boldly claimed that 'by far the greatest part of the property acquired by officers and soldiers in the English force was purchased from the French . . . no officer or soldier in the English force got a single article of intrinsic value from the palace.' This was patently false. In 1861 the French author Victor Hugo wrote a letter in which he described the 'devastation of the Summer Palace' as being 'accomplished by the two victors acting jointly . . . We Europeans are the civilized ones, and for us the Chinese are the barbarians. This is what civilization has done to barbarism.' Here we see on full display the new Enlightenment critique of civilization aping barbarism. That same year, Vincent Scully, a member of the British Liberal Party, declared in Parliament that the destruction of the summer palace 'was an act of barbarism and vandalism' for which it was 'difficult to find any precedent in ancient or modern history, and the nearest resemblance to which was the burning of Persepolis under somewhat similar circumstances by Alexander the Great'.[31]

A similar scene, framed by similar critics, appeared forty years later during the Boxer War. This time, however, it was not just two but eight foreign empires (including the Japanese) that had joined the fray in China in order to punish the court for its support of a violent peasant uprising that targeted foreigners. From July to October 1900, soldiers from all eight empires looted not only the countryside and major cities such as Tianjin and Beijing but the Forbidden City itself, which had been spared during the Second Opium War. On this occasion, the plunder was so brazen, so widespread and so unapologetic that even foreigners living within China – not just armchair critics back home in Europe and America – were horrified at what their countrymen had done. The editors of the *North-China Herald*, an English-language newspaper published in Shanghai, declared, 'it will be a shock to the modern sentiment of the civilised world if such orgies . . . are to be the regular thing. Wherein will the much-boasted civilisation of the West appear if such deeds are the outcome of it?' Though Chinese belligerents were still described as 'savages', readers were reminded that

> it is to exterminate this demon, *not imitate him*, that the United Powers of Europe have sent troops, and we shall be much mistaken if the plunder of civilians in the shameless manner depicted does not raise a howl of execration from one end of the civilised world to the other.[32]

To sum up: military plunder appears to be about as old as politics itself. But so too are critiques of military plunder. The only thing that changed is the content of the critique – that is, the rhetorical basis for portraying military plunder as a sign of debased morals. Depending on the time and place, such plunder may have been criticized as an unnecessary provocation of angry gods or conquered subjects, as an indulgent distraction from more important matters of statecraft, or as a mark of civilization regressing into barbarism. This last critique still has legs today, as can be seen in the recent spate of polemical scholarly books and popular media treatments of the fate of the Benin

Bronzes, in which every single distasteful action of a British soldier is held up as an example of the enduring hypocrisy of the Enlightenment conceit in portraying Westerners as the sole standard by which all other 'savages' of the world should be compared.

But if we place modern instances of military plunder into their proper historical context, it becomes clear that the recent spate of vitriol directed at these infamous campaigns has an august pedigree all of its own. There are, however, two novel features of the present critique that go beyond its adoption of the Enlightenment indictment of a descent into barbarism. First, the critiques of our present day and age, unlike those of earlier eras, routinely lump all forms of antiquity acquisition undertaken by Westerners in non-Western lands as acts of plunder virtually indistinguishable from the worst abuses of an army run amok. In this formulation, there is little difference between a British soldier who bayoneted an innocent Chinese peasant and pocketed an imperial vase in Beijing from a German archaeologist who directed tedious excavations of vast quantities of soil in the Egyptian desert with nothing more than a shovel, a purse and a firman. Our ancestors were acutely aware of the difference – that is why they felt compelled to invent benevolent cover stories for their generals in the field but not for anyone else who happened to come into possession of a valuable work of art. To suggest that such distinctions are meaningless constitutes intellectual laziness at best. At worst, it is intellectual dishonesty marshalled in blatant support of a political agenda – hardly a rhetorical innovation to be proud of.

The other novel feature of present critiques is their invocation of the 'nation' to justify calls for the return of artefacts to their lands of origin. This is the idea, so crudely expressed in the John Oliver monologue, that such objects contain within them the 'memories' of an entire nation – and that these nations cannot truly be whole until those memories are returned to them. What most of us don't realize is that the discourse of the nation is just as much a contingent product of our modern era as the wrath of kidnapped deities was to an earlier age. In fact, nearly every scholar who calls for cultural restitution is acutely aware that the 'nation' is a fictional abstraction of modern political elites, who invoke its powerful allure of cultural or ethnic belonging to justify wars, stifle dissent and enrich elites. There is nothing at all natural about a Black lawyer from New York connecting with a white plumber from Houston on the basis of some sort of primordial American bond. Other than paying taxes to the same government and being exposed to similar consumer products and mass media, they have little else in common. There is a reason why American schoolchildren are forced to recite a pledge of allegiance to 'one nation under God, indivisible' every single morning before school begins: if the idea that they are all united by an abstract bond – being American – wasn't repeatedly drummed into their heads for twelve of the most formative years of their lives, belief in the concept of an imaginary nation to which they belonged not only would appear ridiculous, but would wither away in the face of far more meaningful everyday group identities provided by family, work, religion and recreation.

The wealthy elites of history, those who once owned the works of art now being targeted for restitution, would have scoffed at the notion that anyone outside of their narrow ranks could ever stake any sort of legitimate claim on their cherished private possessions. In 1877, seventeen years after the destruction of the Old Summer Palace, the Qing dynasty official Mao Cheng wrote the following poem while reflecting on its fate:

> A Song dynasty book lies in the basket of an old peasant woman,

> a Yuan dynasty painting hangs on the wall of a shepherd's
> hut.
> Do not enquire into the tattered fate of precious pages
> from the sutras,
> for even the *Emperor's Four Treasuries* have scattered in
> the wind.
> An ancient engraved *ding* bronze vessel rusts away in a
> Buddhist hall,
> while merchants peddle treasures from the imperial
> kiln in their stalls.[33]

This is not merely a nostalgic ode of loss – it is far more specific than that. The poem does not lament the cultural injuries suffered by the Chinese nation writ large, but rather the individual indignities suffered by privileged Chinese elites at the hands of their supposed social and economic inferiors *within* China. The incongruous images conjured up by the poet – a young herder's hut with a Yuan painting on the wall, a Song dynasty book in a peasant woman's basket, a street hawker selling porcelain from the imperial kiln – serve to mourn the lost privileges of those Chinese elites who commissioned, hoarded and enjoyed such things by mocking the notion that any other Chinese of a lower economic status was fit to truly appreciate them. It is also a reminder that opportunistic Chinese pilferers wasted little time in joining Western troops in the plunder of vacated imperial parks and palaces – and that the actions of the Chinese herdsman was just as humiliating (perhaps more so) to China's rich and famous than the actions of the foreign soldier.

As late as 1924 the famous Chinese scholar Wang Guowei continued to defend the idea that anything once held by the emperor in one of his many pleasure grounds or palaces could not be confiscated

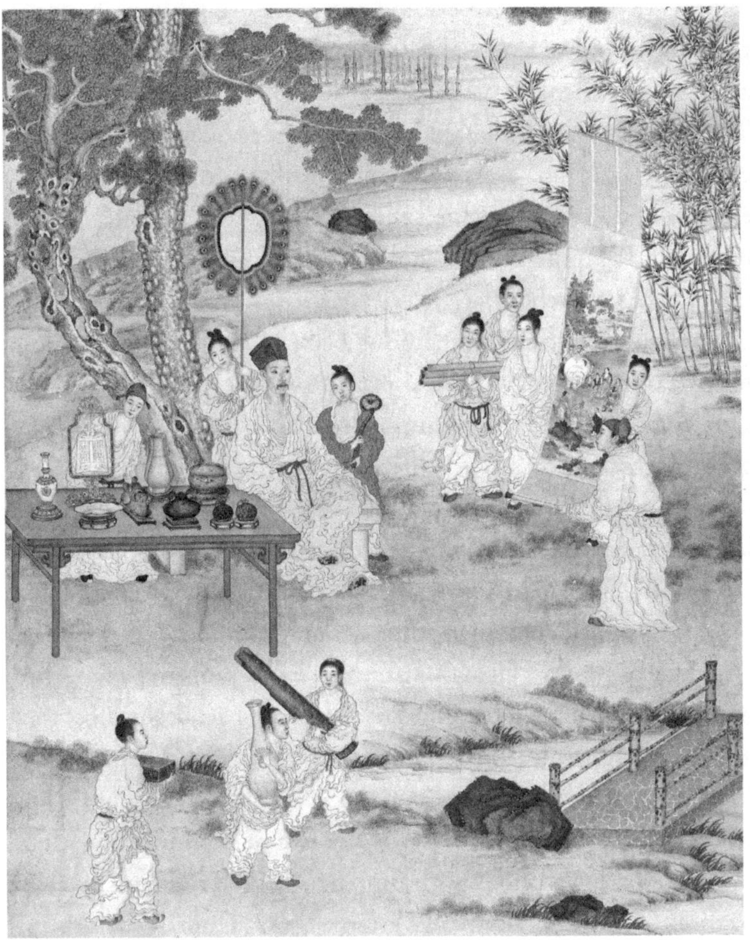

The Qianlong Emperor viewing a painting, detail of a hanging scroll by Giuseppe Castiglione, 18th century.

by the state in the name of the newly imagined Chinese nation. 'Every object in the imperial palace', he wrote, 'under any laws, ancient or modern, Chinese or foreign, is the private property of the imperial family.'[34] The Qianlong Emperor, who reigned for six decades during the eighteenth century and amassed one of the most impressive collections of art and antiquities in Chinese history, probably would have agreed with Wang's assessment. According to art historian Nicole T. C. Chiang, the emperor's collections were 'intentionally chosen and hidden away from public gaze'. The most commonly used phrase to refer to these works of art during the Qing era was *neifu suocang*, which means 'that which is collected or hidden by the imperial household' – and the emperor was head of the imperial household.[35]

Surviving paintings of Qianlong make it abundantly clear just how he interacted with his jealously hoarded art and antiquities. One composition depicts him sitting in leisurely repose while a group of servants carries sealed containers into his presence. These containers hold various works of art, such as the bronzes and porcelain vases already arranged on the table next to him. Another group of servants holds up a painting that they have just unfurled from its previously sealed container. After a couple of minutes or so, once Qianlong has had his fill of this painting, his servants will wrap it up once again and place it back into its container. Eventually, all of the art and antiquities featured in this painting – as well as the painting itself – will be returned to the dark, inaccessible storage room from whence they came. Until, that is, the next time the emperor wishes to gaze upon his precious possessions in splendid isolation for two or three minutes – or until a Western soldier, Chinese 'herdsboy' or Chinese peasant takes advantage of sudden political instability to claim it for themselves and turn a modest profit by selling it on the antiquities market.

In fact, once we liberate our minds from the ideological prison of imaginary nations, it is not entirely outrageous to suggest that the first time any of the exquisite works of Chinese art depicted in this painting actually proved beneficial in any way to the common man was when they were forcibly removed from the emperor's luxurious palace or pleasure grounds by a poorly educated Western soldier or illiterate Chinese peasant during a time of upheaval. When we assume that ancient works of art once somehow represented collective nations that simply did not exist at the time of their creation, we are swallowing twentieth-century propaganda wholesale.

One way to test the notion that art and antiquities were regarded as symbols of the 'nations' whose blood, sweat and taxes allegedly supported their production is to identify the point at which besieged rulers began to take their collections with them any time they felt compelled to flee for their lives. As it happens, we have some excellent case studies in China that will help to shed some light on this question. In 1860, when the Xianfeng Emperor abandoned Beijing and took refuge in Manchuria during the Second Opium War, he left behind nearly all of the art and antiquities in his many collections in the Forbidden City and Old Summer Palace. In fact, it was precisely because the emperor did not regard the cultural treasures of the Old Summer Palace as an integral component of his right to rule over his Chinese subjects that they became so vulnerable to British and French armies. In explaining his decision to set fire to the Old Summer Palace, Lord Elgin wrote that it was a punishment that 'would fall, not on the people, who may be comparatively innocent, but exclusively on the Emperor, whose direct personal responsibility for the crime committed is established'.[36] In other words, both Elgin and the Xianfeng Emperor regarded the Old Summer Palace – and everything in it – to be a symbol of the emperor himself, not of the Chinese nation. If Elgin had wanted to punish the Chinese 'nation' rather than the emperor, the last thing he would have targeted was the emperor's exclusive imperial playground and private possessions, which no Chinese commoner had ever laid eyes on before.

A similar episode was re-enacted yet again in 1900 during the Boxer War, when Xianfeng's once low-ranking consort Cixi – now the powerful Empress Dowager – also fled Beijing, this time westward to Xi'an. She, too, left the treasures of the Forbidden City to fend for themselves, with predictable results. But the important point here is that neither Xianfeng nor Cixi felt that the abandonment of these exquisite works of art to invading armies would endanger their claims to political legitimacy upon their return to the capital. The only downside for them would be that they would simply have several thousand fewer antiquities to take out of storage from time to time to gaze at for a minute or two in splendid isolation while sipping tea and munching on any number of delicacies – delicacies which probably cost several months' worth of wages for the vast majority of their subjects.

Fast forward just three decades later, however, and we find a very different response among Chinese leaders. In 1933 the Nationalist government of Chiang Kai-shek, anticipating Japanese plunder of the Forbidden City upon the inevitable fall of Beijing to their armies, shipped nearly 20,000 crates of art and antiquities south to Shanghai for safekeeping. When Shanghai fell as well, all these crates were transported – at great expense, hardship and significant danger to the antiquities themselves – over thousands of kilometres and many years to fortified caves located deep within the interior of China. In 1938, however, at the same time that these newly reimagined symbols of the Chinese nation were being given the white glove treatment, Chiang ordered the deliberate destruction of the dikes on the Yellow River as a means of impeding the Japanese advance. The resulting floods are estimated to have killed up to 1 million Chinese peasants – a tragic and heartless demonstration of the grossly inflated political value now placed upon all these ancient paintings and bronzes, to the point where they were now considered more valuable than the actual lives of the Chinese people they were supposed to represent. And Chiang's obsession didn't stop with the surrender of the Japanese: in 1949, as the Chinese Communists forced the Nationalists to flee the mainland, Chiang took the cream of the crop with him to Taiwan. Before long, these well-travelled works of art were enshrined in a brand new National Palace Museum in Taipei, in an attempt to lend cultural substance to his government's farcical occupation of the China seat at the United Nations for the next two decades.[37]

All this is not to say that the ill-gotten fruits of military plunder lack any moral basis for return to their lands of origin today. But let us not pretend that any such returns will serve to rectify the supposed and so-called historical injustice of nations being deprived of their memories. The Western plunder of Chinese antiquities occurred long before Chiang Kai-shek's megalomaniacal elevation of the hidden treasures of long-reviled emperors over the lives of a million of his own citizens. Instead, every single instance of such plunder occurred at a time when almost no one, either inside or outside China, regarded these antiquities as symbols of the Chinese nation – such ideas were decades in the future. Instead, let us undertake their return because military plunder was the one and only form of relocated artwork throughout history that involved the use of blood-spattered swords and firearms and did not involve the voluntary consent of any native stakeholders. It was, we might say, the one and only means of Western collecting in foreign lands that could not be stopped simply by saying no.

2

DEALERS

For most people today, Indiana Jones is the spitting archetype of a Western archaeologist. He travels to exotic and dangerous lands, uses his wits to recover rare and wonderful artefacts and then returns home to put them in museums. But what most fans of this famous film franchise don't realize is that Jones's most iconic line – 'That belongs in a museum!' – was not uttered until the third film, *Indiana Jones and the Last Crusade* (1989). Not only that, but during an early brainstorming session in 1978 for the first film, George Lucas revealed that his original vision for the protagonist was as a much less savoury 'bounty hunter for antiquities' or a 'grave robber for hire', one who just happened to turn such shady activities into 'a very lucrative profession'.[1] Indeed, despite some minor tweaks by screenwriter Larry Kasdan to the first script, the Indiana Jones portrayed on screen bears far more resemblance to a dealer than an archaeologist. In fact, all of the most memorable artefacts sought out by Dr Jones in the first three films – the Golden Idol, Ark of the Covenant, Urn of Nurhaci and Holy Grail – are presented as paid commissions, which Jones pursues only reluctantly in order to please his wealthy and mysterious patrons.[2]

Real-life archaeologists in history hardly ever worked on commission to recover specific artefacts. Quite the contrary; their days were filled with the tedious and anxious pursuit of funding from a variety of organizations including governments, universities and foundations, all of which have scarce funds to disburse among a bounty of applicants. Instead of the single-minded pursuit of a quasi-historical object made famous by biblical bedtime stories, an archaeologist is much more likely to apply for funds to undertake a broadly defined search for material evidence of Judeo-Assyrian cultural interaction in Mesopotamia during the Bronze Age. On the rare occasions they are lucky enough to be bankrolled by an eccentric tycoon, the alleviation of financial hardship is usually offset by the unpredictable and vainglorious demands of their private patron. This was certainly the case with the Egyptologist Howard Carter, who found it impossible to put a stop to the revolving door of friends, relatives and reporters that the Earl of Carnarvon, his patron, imposed upon him while attempting to catalogue the glittering treasures found in the tomb of Tutankhamun in early 1923.

Our collective inability to distinguish a dealer from an archaeologist continues right up to the present day. A few years ago, I received a phone call from a customs agent who worked for the National Security Administration (NSA). He wanted to know if I would be willing to help the U.S. government scrutinize a questionable shipment of ancient Chinese porcelain to determine whether or not its contents were authentic, and if so, how old the pieces might be. It felt like a much less glamorous version of the scene in *Raiders of the Lost Ark* (1981), the first Indiana Jones film, where two smartly dressed men from Army Intelligence enlist Indiana Jones to help them find the Ark of the Covenant before the Nazis can. I told the NSA agent that he needed to find a dealer, not a historian; I could only tell him about the rise and fall of the famous porcelain production site at Jingdezhen during the Qing dynasty (1644–1911), along with the economic transport links that facilitated its trade throughout East Asia and beyond. But if he wanted to know the composition of the pigment used, the temperature at which the kilns were fired and other highly specialized technical details that might point to a forgery, he would have to ask a dealer.

In other words, the professional skill set and training of a dealer and a historian are quite distinct from one another and are applied to very different purposes. It makes more sense to think of various Western collectors of non-Western art in terms of the professions they represented. The beneficiaries of gifts tended to be diplomats (or at least someone temporarily acting in a diplomatic capacity), while plunder was carried out by soldiers. Archaeologists, who often began their careers as historians or philologists, were scholars. We will examine them in the next chapter. Dealers are best described not as scholars, but rather as businessmen. Their goal was to turn as large a profit as possible from the sale of art and antiquities to well-heeled customers. And if the highest-paying customer just happened to live in another country, so be it. Just like multinational corporations today, a dealer's desire to reach as many customers as possible fostered a cosmopolitan worldview in which anyone who was both able and willing to purchase the dealer's products would be welcomed into an exclusive club of like-minded consumers defined not by their national, cultural or ethnic origins, but rather by their common love of the same product – in this case, art and antiquities.

To put it another way, dealers have always been far less imprisoned by nationalist propaganda than the rest of us – after all, their livelihoods depend upon it. By contrast, scholars and diplomats have the unfortunate habit of describing the art and antiquities they covet as 'priceless'. This is because they nearly always discuss such objects within the context of the nations and states that claim these objects today. And since these nations and states often base their modern claims to political legitimacy upon physical possession and display of the material remains of the past, these remains must be regarded as priceless, making anyone who tries to remove them a thief or a traitor. But to dealers, no artefact is priceless; if it was, they'd be out of business. Instead, dealers treat the material remains of the past as saleable commodities that must be shrewdly marketed to a wealthy clientele. This clientele is small but influential, chiefly consisting of two types of customers: tycoons who want to build a private collection and museums who want to build a public collection. A third type of customer – foreign tourists looking for a memorable souvenir – are far less likely to acquire anything deemed worthy of display on a pedestal.

Another reason we often confuse dealers for scholars is because many scholars known for their excavations and expeditions also bought and sold antiquities on the side to generate a supplemental income. Though Giovanni Belzoni did indeed donate the Memnon Head to the British Museum, he also collected many other cultural artefacts that he turned over to various British customers for a fee. Perhaps the most famous is the so-called Philae Obelisk, which Belzoni helped transport all the way to a rural English estate from an island temple complex in Upper Egypt. The British Egyptologist Flinders Petrie, famous for his decades of meticulous excavations, is nonetheless believed to have purchased anywhere from 35 to 45 per cent of the antiquities he removed from Egypt.[3] And long before Howard Carter achieved global celebrity through his association with the tomb of Tutankhamun, he was better known in Egypt as a shrewd antiquities dealer from whom wealthy foreign tourists and major museums could acquire authentic, high-quality artefacts. His standard commission was 15 per cent. In northwestern China, the British archaeologist Aurel Stein regularly bought Buddhist antiquities from a local dealer in the oasis of Khotan before he embarked on his own long-distance expeditions to acquire even more of the same. During the first half of the twentieth century, the famous Chinese antiquarian Luo Zhenyu supported his independent scholarship on the recently excavated oracle bones by selling other works of art in his possession to anyone – Chinese, Western or Japanese – willing to pay top dollar.

Diplomats, soldiers and scholars may captivate the public imagination and hoard all the media attention, but it seems clear that dealers accounted for the lion's share of art and antiquities acquired by most Western museums. As such, it is imperative that we come to a better understanding of the cultural, economic and legal conditions that allowed dealers to flourish for so long. First, above all

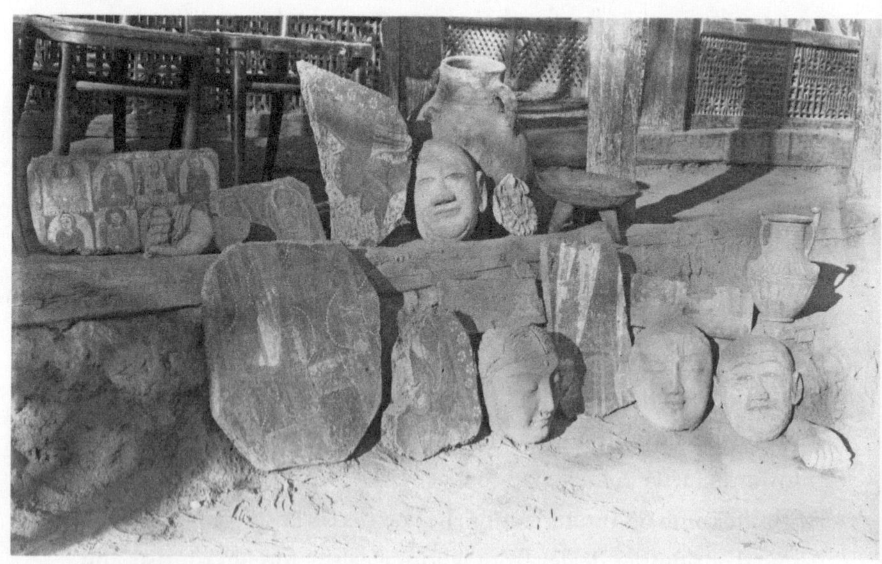

Antiquities shop with Buddhist artefacts, Khotan, Xinjiang, 1922.

else, dealers can only exist where there are customers. And these customers must identify in some way with the commodities on sale. Such an identification often comes in the form of a perception of cultural continuity: for example, Europeans who bought an ancient Egyptian funerary papyrus in Luxor must have already been convinced – by newspapers, school curricula, public exhibitions, novels, tourist brochures and so on – that the people of ancient Egypt were members of their preferred genealogy of the history of Western civilization. Such a view did not become commonplace until the French scholar Jean-François Champollion deciphered the ancient Egyptian hieroglyphs in 1822 with the aid of the Rosetta Stone. At that point, ancient Egypt joined all the other pre-Islamic cultures of the Near East in being perceived by European scholars as possible influences on the most cherished ancestors of all: the Greeks and Romans.

The only other place in the world where a perception of cultural continuity with the material remains of antiquity could give rise to a modern network of antiquity dealers was in China. There, the antiquities trade far pre-dated the arrival of Westerners, with Chinese scholars regularly engaging thousands of years of ancient scholarship by comparing classic Confucian, Buddhist and Daoist texts with newly unearthed bronze vessels, stone steles and inscribed bamboo slips, among many other types of artefacts. In a famous eighteenth-century copy of a Song dynasty painting titled *Along the River during the Qingming Festival,* an attentive viewer can spot an outdoor antiquities market where wealthy Chinese customers point in awe at hanging scrolls and closely inspect bronzes vessels and porcelain wares. Thus in China, with its long history of treating art and antiquities as saleable commodities, we will have the additional luxury of being able to examine the cultural and legal assumptions upon which the antiquities trade flourished well before the arrival of any Western customers.

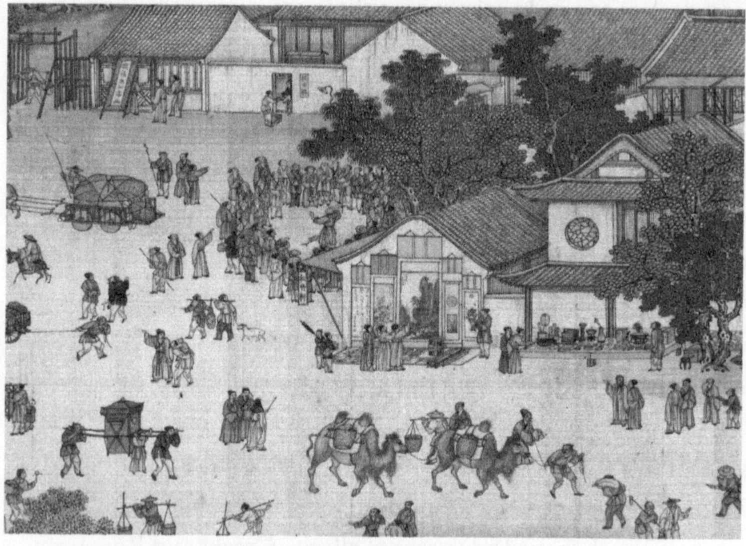

A Chinese antiquities market before the arrival of Western collectors, detail of the handscroll *Along the River during the Qingming Festival* (Qing court version), 1736.

We have already seen how early twentieth-century Chinese scholars were fond of invoking a stock phrase to describe any antiquity newly unearthed from the soil: 'the earth does not love its treasures' (*di bu ai bao*). This word choice is deliberate. Whereas most of us have been conditioned to believe that subterranean cultural treasures are the property of the nation in which they are found, the premodern Chinese view was quite different. To them, it was the earth that owned these treasures. But once the earth relinquished its hold on them and they were 'struck by the light of day' – as the expression continues – 'they supply lovers of antiquity and connoisseurs of the marvellous'. Nowhere in this formulation is there the sense that anyone subsisting above ground has a prior claim on what lies underground, either before or after it emerges from the soil. Anyone can claim these treasures. Not only that, but it was assumed that any given collection would continue to pass through many unrelated private hands over the course of history. The Qing dynasty collector Qiang Yong once observed that while the acquisition of calligraphy and paintings was 'an elegant affair', such objects were 'not indispensable'. Instead, he likened them to

> clouds and mist passing before one's eyes. They may pass by but not stay. If one is reluctant to let go, covetousness grows and turns the elegant affair into vulgarity. Examining collectors throughout history, no one has been able to pass down his collection to posterity who still manages to hold onto it after hundreds of years.[4]

This is a radically different view from our popular understandings of art and antiquities today. To us, these 'priceless' objects are permanent, inalienable symbols of the cultural nations they are presumed to represent. To Qiang and his Chinese contemporaries, however, it was taken for granted that such things would pass from collector to collector in the same way that clouds and mist might dissipate and reappear. Either the earth owned them or a person owned them; abstract entities such as nations did not. And when they changed hands and found a new owner, no one regarded this change in ownership as theft. It was simply a matter of one owner transferring his claim to another owner upon mutually agreed terms.

There was, however, an important exception to this general rule, and it concerned tombs. In fact, most civilizations throughout history have professed adherence to some sort of regulation that criminalizes the unauthorized excavation of tombs. Most of the time, these laws were created to deter the plunder of tombs that contained the corpses and goods of the recently deceased – not the long-forgotten corpses of people who lived hundreds or even thousands of years ago. This distinction is perhaps best illustrated by the sixth-century pronouncement of Theodoric the Great, king of the Ostrogoths, who told his followers that it was okay to take things from graves so long as no human remains were disturbed. After all, 'it is not greedy to take what no owner can complain of having lost.'[5] In China, where the tombs of ancestors were considered particularly sacred and punishments for their disturbance harsh, peasants nonetheless regularly stumbled upon the graves of ancient elites and claimed their goods for themselves. During the Song dynasty (960–1279), the enforcement of the prohibition against tomb raiding in such cases was lax and capricious: occasionally a zealous local official might arrest the perpetrators, but most were content to accept a portion of plundered grave goods themselves as gifts, with some even regifting them to the emperor himself or to other high-ranking officials.[6]

These were the cultural, economic and legal conditions that facilitated the business activities of dealers. The contents of newly discovered ancient tombs for which no identifiable descendant was alive to submit a complaint were fair game. Forgotten antiquities buried beneath the soils of the earth were also fair game. And privately owned works of art whose owners wished to sell their valuable possessions for cash or other forms of economic capital were definitely fair game. As for customers, anyone who identified in some way with the artistic wares on sale in a dealer's inventory – and had the money to pay – was a potential client, regardless of nationality. The only people who would be considered thieves in this enterprise were those who took things without permission from identifiable owners (or in the case of tombs, identifiable descendants). Such understandings would govern the activities of antiquity dealers from their earliest days until the second decade of the twentieth century.

As we will see, it is at that point – 1912 in Egypt, 1914 in China – that a new series of momentous antiquities laws were passed into legislation. These laws had the effect of elevating the state, as guardian of the 'nation', to the status of a new de facto owner of all art and antiquities found within its borders, with major consequences for dealers.

Let us begin with Egypt. What did the dealer network there look like, and how did its supply chain operate? According to Egyptologists Fredrik Hagen and Kim Ryholt, approximately 90 per cent of all profits made in the dealer trade occurred in Cairo and Luxor.[7] These were the two cities that every tourist visited, and they also happened to be located in close proximity to the majority of ancient tombs and monuments. Dealers conducted nearly all of their business during the four winter months, when temperatures were more suitable for Western tourists. The supply chain began in outlying rural areas, where the poor peasants known as *fellahin* routinely supplemented their fields with *sebakh*: fertilizer derived from the crumbling remains of ancient monuments. As with the obelisks gifted away by successive Egyptian pashas, these ruins served no other functional purpose for the local residents, being regarded – if they were regarded at all – as the abode of jinns (genies) or sprites who may be guarding a cache of gold underneath. When both jinns and gold consistently failed to materialize, the *fellahin* took the initiative to turn worthless heaps of stone and papyri into an economic commodity by using them as a substitute for costly fertilizer.

What changed during the nineteenth century was the rising value of this fertilizer substitute. With the translation of the Rosetta Stone in 1822 and the incorporation of ancient Egypt into the selective narrative of Western civilization – as a precursor to ancient Greece – Western museums and wealthy elites were all eager to acquire their

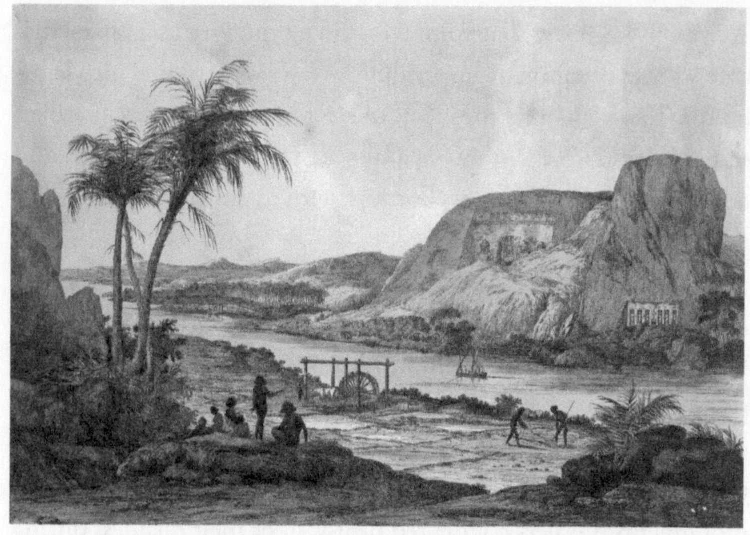

Egyptian peasants farming in close proximity to the two temples at Abu Simbel, 1820, engraving by Agostino Aglio.

own piece of the pharaonic pie. Fortunately, there was more than enough for everyone, and everyone seemed willing to play his or her part in the supply chain with enthusiasm. *Fellahin* were so eager to supplement their meagre agricultural incomes by selling portable antiquities that the British scholar Archibald Sayce was moved to observe that *fellahin* and 'antiquities hunters' are 'two synonymous terms'. In 1892 the popular Baedeker's guidebook for Egypt informed its readers that 'half the population of Luxor is engaged in traffic with antiquities.'[8]

At the bottom of the dealer hierarchy were local *fellahin* who both uncovered and then personally peddled their goods to any Western traveller who happened to pass through major transport hubs or ruins. In 1899 the Danish Egyptologist H. O. Lange described the opportunistic nature of such transactions as he boarded a ferry across the Nile at Qena:

> Among these [passengers] there were some farmers from the other side, who tried to sell me antiquities. One young man offered me a silver ring which he had on his finger, in which a scarab had been set; he valued the scarab at 2 shillings and the ring at 1. A distinguished old man in a brown camel hair coat then dragged forth an apron-like piece of cloth, and from the individually tied corners he pulled out various small objects that he wanted me to buy, but I conducted no trade on this occasion.[9]

More reliable, but less lucrative profits could be had by selling objects such as these not to a foreigner, but rather to an agent of an urban dealer who was based in Cairo or Luxor. In their list of dealers mentioned in the Lange papers, Hagen and Ryholt identify more than 250 dealers throughout the country, most of whom were Egyptian. In addition, there were Greeks, Armenians, Turks and Europeans, many of whom entered the antiquities trade as a side hustle to supplement the income of another career. They came from all walks of life, from destitute *fellahin* and modest textile merchants to privileged consuls and resourceful missionaries. One dealer was an American gynaecologist who got involved with the trade after treating *fellahin* patients who had stumbled upon ancient papyri while scrounging for *sebakh*.[10]

At the upper end of the market were prominent urban dealers who managed a permanent shop next to the major hotels for foreign visitors and residents in Cairo and Luxor. They usually had English or French signs, could conduct business in European languages and offered other high-end amenities not found among the freelance dealers, such as allowing purchases on credit, issuing certificates of authenticity and the right to a full refund if the piece turned out to be less than advertised. Of course, all these amenities came at a grossly inflated price, which is why these dealers targeted only the wealthiest customers near the luxurious Shepheard's Hotel or Continental Hotel in Cairo. When geopolitical crises such as the Boer War (1899) broke out and stemmed the flow of foreign travellers to Egypt, these shops felt the financial pinch and longed for the return of big spenders. One customer who was sorely missed was Sir Wallis Budge, the head of the Egyptian Department at the British Museum, who had to cancel his regularly scheduled purchasing trip in 1899 due to an eye ailment. In order to plan for such setbacks, the most resourceful dealers would open up branch shops in Paris, London or New York so they could take their wares directly to the most lucrative customers.

What are we to make of all this? First, it seems clear that the antiquities trade in Egypt during the nineteenth century was a simple fact

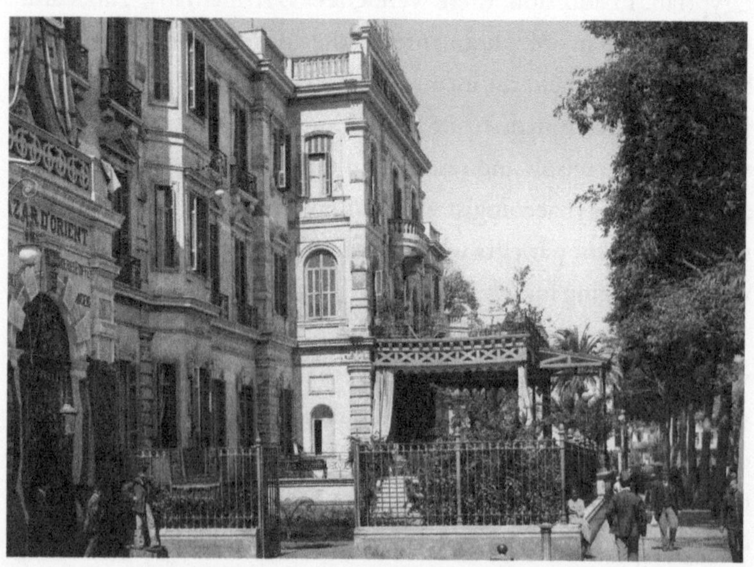

Bazar d'Orient at Shepheard's Hotel, Cairo, *c.* 1900.

of life for a substantial percentage of the population. Pretty much anyone who could get their hands on an ancient artefact found a way to peddle it to foreigners. There is no evidence that the *fellahin* who supplied dealers with their stock (or any of the dealers themselves, for that matter) believed that they were engaged in an immoral act of theft from the 'Egyptian nation'. How could they, when the curators of the national museum in Cairo themselves openly sold antiquities to the general public? In 1888 the premier national museum in Egypt – then known as the Gizeh Museum and later as the Egyptian Museum – opened up a Sales Room (Salle de Vente) within the main hall for the explicit purpose of peddling surplus antiquities to anyone who visited the museum. Operated by the government-funded Antiquities Service, the Sales Room was designed to generate funds for both the museum and its archaeological digs. Indeed, some digs were initiated for the sole purpose of finding portable artefacts that could be sold in the Sales Room. All such purchases came with a guarantee of authenticity and an export permit.[11]

So not only did nearly everyone in Egypt want a piece of the lucrative pharaonic pie – from the most erudite of scholars to the poorest of illiterate peasants – but the pie itself was so incredibly large that even the director of the Antiquities Service himself felt that it was entirely appropriate to devise creative new ways of turning excess supply into ready cash. Even H. O. Lange, whom Hagen and Ryholt describe as 'a man with strong moral principles' who regularly campaigned against alcohol consumption back home in Denmark, 'seems to have been less concerned with the ethics of trade in antiquities than one might have expected'. And when he did give vent to a sense of moral frustration, it was to lament the 'immeasurable' damage 'done to science'.[12] This, in fact, was the most common critique levelled against Egyptian dealers and their supply chain throughout the

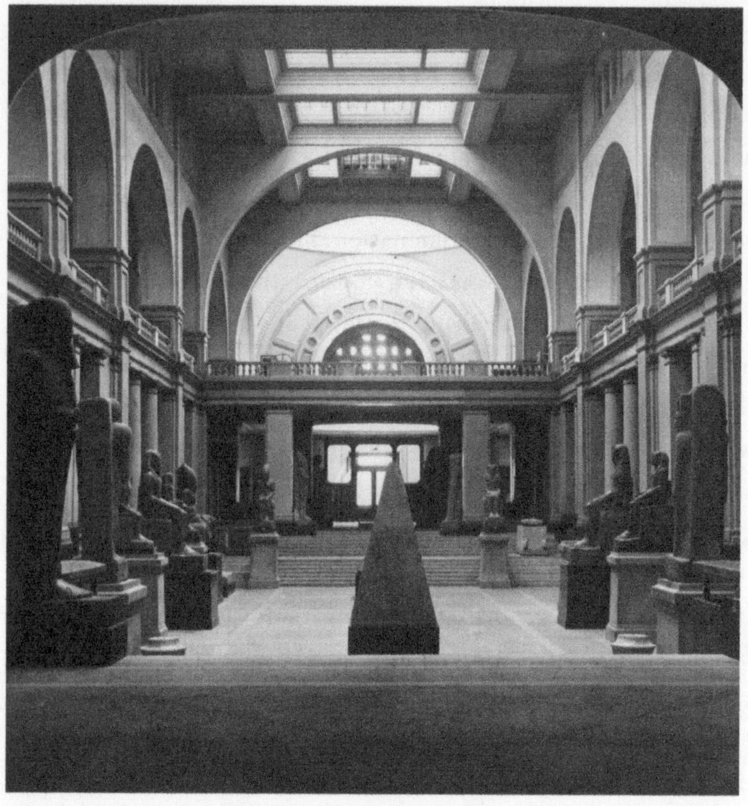

Interior of the Museum of Egyptian Antiquities, Cairo, *c.* 1908.

country during the nineteenth and early twentieth centuries, and it is a discourse that is still with us today any time an ancient site is said to be 'plundered' by 'tomb raiders' and 'grave robbers'.

And yet, as we have already seen on several occasions, the moment we look beyond the ideological prison of nationalism it becomes possible to undertake a long overdue re-evaluation of the historical context within which those who aided and abetted the movement of art and antiquities across ethnic and cultural borders operated. The supposedly nefarious role of those at the bottom of the dealer supply chain is a case in point. The very terms used to describe them – 'tomb raiders', 'grave robbers', 'illicit diggers' – presuppose a sense of criminal guilt and moral culpability. So who created these terms and for what purposes? Certainly not the *fellahin* or the dealers who bought their serendipitous finds. Before an 'antiquities-hunter' can be branded a criminal, there must be a plausible victim who is imagined to suffer from the crime. But since no one in Egypt could claim plausible ownership of the ancient pharaonic ruins (beyond their utility as fertilizer), such a victim could only be invented in the abstract.

To Western scholars, both those who worked within the Egyptian Antiquities Service and those who worked for foreign institutions, this abstract victim was science. To the small number of Western-educated Egyptian scholars who were also employed by the Egyptian government, there was yet another abstract victim: the Egyptian nation. Though they seem distinct, these two victims were frequently invoked in tandem, since the interests of nations – or, in the case of Westerners, their empires – were often said to be advanced by the scientific study of the material resources of our world. Today, most of us have been conditioned to sympathize with these two abstract victims, and we are quick to parrot the lofty discourse – initially peddled by only the tiniest percentage of our most wealthy and powerful ancestors – about defending the interests of science and nation. But in so doing, we are re-enacting in the present day their historical exploitation and oppression of the poorest members of society, all in the name of a supposed higher good.

Once we sift through the misleading discourse concerning both science and nation, a better way to conceptualize the origins of pejorative labels such as 'illicit diggers' begins to emerge: as a product of class tensions. In other words, Western and domestic elites habitually used the advantages of their education and wealth to criminalize the poor for being poor. In these damning formulations, the poor were guilty of betraying the elite interests of science, the nation, or both. But for those who could not afford to obtain a proper education, these elite abstractions merely constituted a bizarre and confounding pretext to deny them the hard-won fruits of their labour. From the perspective of a poor and often illiterate peasant, the lucrative supply chain that ended in a dealer's shop was a tangible form of wealth redistribution. To any Egyptian who had not received a Western education, the dealer – domestic or foreign – was nothing short of a magician: with a mysterious sleight of hand, previously worthless objects were somehow transformed into freely given cash from the wealthiest members of society to the poorest. Not only that, but anyone, no matter how poor or ordinary, could try their hand at these profitable magic tricks. Lange once recalled an Egyptian freelance dealer named Mansur, who had an 'unbelievable number of pockets out of which he pulls his treasures, and again and again one thinks that this has got to be the last, but there is still more'.[13]

Today, some scholars, cognizant of the elitist origins of labels that criminalize the survivalist strategies of the poor and disenfranchised, prefer to describe impoverished antiquities hunters as 'subsistence diggers' rather than 'tomb robbers' or 'illicit diggers'.[14] This new label draws attention to the economic imperatives that motivate such activities rather than to the impossibly high standards against which educated elites attempt to measure the moral guilt of those who do not have the luxury of adhering to expensive abstract principles. But 'subsistence diggers' is a phrase generally invoked only to criticize entrenched power structures of our own day. I suggest that we should apply it as well to the many near-destitute antiquities hunters who participated in the supply chain of any given dealer network throughout the nineteenth and early twentieth centuries. Once we strip away the moral hypocrisy of educated elites, it quickly becomes apparent that hardly anyone else in Egypt felt even the slightest twinge of moral regret at dealers and their supply chain. The fact that business transactions involving antiquities were completed at all, writes Hagen and Ryholt, 'indicates that the terms (and monetary values) involved were acceptable to both parties'. In fact, they continue, those who acted in the capacity of a dealer – from opportunistic *fellahin* to successful shop merchants – 'may very well have felt that they came away from the exchanges with the upper hand'.[15]

The fact that poor, illiterate peasants and minimally educated shopkeepers were turning a handsome profit at the expense of the lofty scientific and nationalist ideals of Western and Egyptian elites was an intolerable state of affairs to anyone with the education and leisure to think about it. But most of the time, there was little they could do about it – the economic motivation to supplement paltry, unsustainable incomes was so strong that most antiquities hunters were willing to brave not only the deadly heat of the summer, when no Western archaeologist in his right mind would undertake an excavation, but the treacherous conditions of dark, subterranean tombs in the wee hours of the night with little more than a threadbare rope, a rusty spade and their wits.

In the event that these subsistence diggers happened to uncover a particularly impressive collection of antiquities, however, the educated elites were quick to pounce. This happened in 1871, when two brothers from the el-Rasul family discovered a spectacular cache of New Kingdom royal mummies and their burial goods in a hidden shaft not far from the Valley of the Kings near Luxor. When objects from their sarcophagi began to appear on the open market, both Western and Egyptian members of the Antiquities Service in Cairo embarked on a ten-year witch hunt to identify and arrest those responsible. In the end, both brothers were imprisoned, with rumours that one had been beaten and the other tortured in order to obtain the location of the shaft. All this was done so that the Antiquities Service itself could take control of the treasures and place them inside glass cabinets in the museum in Cairo, thereby depriving the el-Rasul family of a precious opportunity to escape the abject poverty of the Luxor desert. Meanwhile, a veritable red carpet of antiquities was made available to European elites. In 1857 Said Pasha prepared for the cousin of French emperor Napoleon III's visit to Egypt by instructing Auguste Mariette, the French director of the Antiquities Service, to ensure that 'every step of the visiting prince' would 'sprout antiquities'. Mariette did as he was told, taking objects from several different sites throughout Egypt and reburying them for the excavation staged for the French prince.[16]

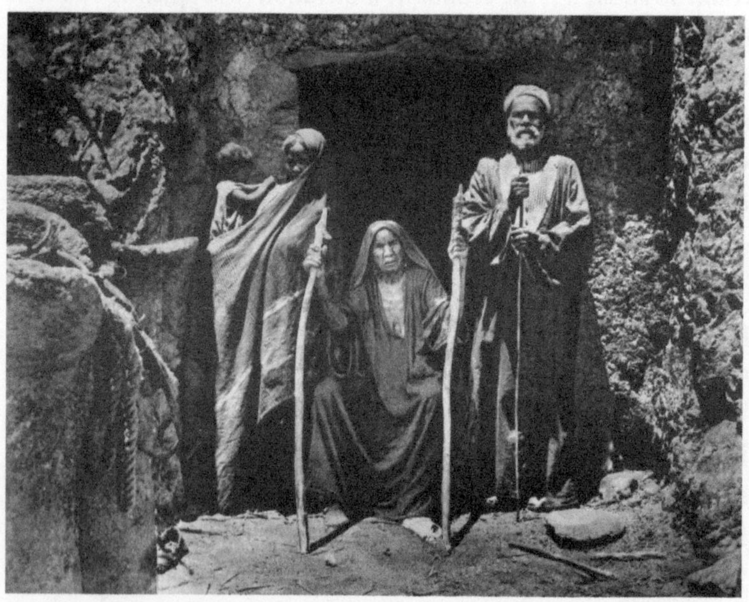

Subsistence digger Abd el-Rasul with his family, *c.* 1909.

A century later, the Western-educated Egyptian film-maker Shadi Abdel Salam directed the Arabic-language film *al-Mummia* (1969), known in English as *The Night of Counting the Years.* The film portrays a fictionalized version of the el-Rasul brothers' discovery and its aftermath, with heroic Egyptian scholars in Cairo setting out to track down the location of this ancient royal cache in an attempt to recover the lost voice and identities of their collective ancestors. The el-Rasul clan, here fictionalized as the Hurabat tribe, is portrayed in an unflattering light, backstabbing one another for immoral profit, consorting with shady dealers and prostitutes, and generally serving as a foil for anything that does not conform with the film-maker's nationalist, Western-inspired vision of what a modern, scientific Egypt should look like.[17]

To add insult to injury, about the same time that the el-Rasul brothers were being beaten and tortured in prison for the benefit of Western science and the Egyptian nation, the Gizeh Museum in Cairo opened its Sales Room in order to turn a bald profit from the museum's excess supply of antiquities. The message could not be clearer: when privileged elites chose to sell antiquities for cash it could only be for the benefit of the world, but when impoverished peasants did the same it was a selfish act that undermined scientific and national progress. The same critique was levelled at the illiterate Daoist priest Wang Yuanlu by educated Chinese elites in the early twentieth century after he discovered and then sold the majority of the contents of the secret cave library at the Mogao Grottoes. But Wang, destitute and uneducated, saw his discovery as an economic stroke of good luck that could be used to magically transform otherwise useless objects into cash for the renovation of nearby temples.

Although Chinese, Western and Egyptian elites alike all invoked higher abstract discourses to justify their critiques of peasants like the el-Rasul brothers and Wang Yuanlu, underneath their rhetorical bluster was a pragmatic business sensibility that often regarded antiquities in terms of value that were eerily similar to those of dealers and antiquities hunters. In 1907, while engaged in tense negotiations with Aurel Stein over the amount of money he would 'donate' to Wang's temple in exchange for thousands of ancient manuscripts from Cave 17, Wang decided to drop all pretence of a lofty discourse. According to Stein's field diary, while Wang began the day by clamouring for a '"subscription" to the temple', he ended the day with 'lengthy negotiations on plain trade basis'.[18] In an echo of such language, in 1912 Arthur Weigall, the chief inspector of antiquities for Upper Egypt, submitted a proposal to the national museum in Cairo to vastly increase the number and quality of antiquities offered for sale to the general public through the Sales Room, and to put its dealings on plain 'business lines'. He complained that 'dealers in Egypt make enormous profits each year by the sale of antiquities' while the museum made only 'very small profits'. He could not stand the fact that 'the dealers are thus without competition, and all persons who are engaged in buying antiquities for foreign museums or collections go always to them, and never come to us.'[19]

Weigall's business proposal was not adopted. Instead, the Antiquities Service had a better plan: a new law that would require all dealers to register with the Antiquities Service and obtain an official licence in order to sell antiquities. When this ambitious idea became law in 1912, it immediately criminalized the supplementary side hustles that had sustained the precarious livelihoods of rural communities throughout Egypt. Now, 'every antiquity found on, or in the ground, shall belong to the Public Domain of the State.' And the state itself arrogated the sole power to determine which dealers were legitimate and which were not. In the end, just over one hundred dealers successfully secured an official licence. This licence required them to keep all of their inventory on hand in a designated shop, which could be inspected at any time for evidence of purchases from freelance antiquities hunters. Anyone who now tried to collect antiquities on their own free time and sell them either to an urban dealer or directly to tourists risked imprisonment and fines.

This was class warfare. From the perspective of most Egyptians, who lived in crushing rural poverty, it was an attempt by Western and Egyptian political elites to impose a state monopoly on an abundant natural resource once freely available to anyone willing to work for it. By all accounts, the *fellahin* did everything in their limited power to undermine the imposition of this monopoly. The Egyptologist Reginald Engelbach characterized the expression of these class tensions as a humorous game of cat-and-mouse. 'The prospect of a reward out of all proportion to the labour expended in getting it,' he wrote in 1924, 'the fun of dodging the policeman and the slight element of risk . . . all combine to make illicit excavation the most delightful sport which the country can offer the *fellah*.' Though the situation may have seemed like fun and games to the well-fed, well-educated and well-paid Engelbach, it was a serious matter to the malnourished peasants, who now found their livelihoods under attack. *Fellahin* who spent time in prison for flouting the new law wore their incarceration as a badge of honour, as was the case with Abu Lifa, who was described by one traveller as 'the anteekeh man of his region, [who] has been in prison for it, which seems to add to a man's reputation.'[20]

The 1912 antiquities law did not put an end to the industrious activities of Egypt's subsistence diggers. It simply made these activities that much more dangerous. In 1922 H. E. Winlock, the assistant curator at the Metropolitan Museum of Art in New York, published a story told to him by a prominent Luxor dealer named Mohammed

Mohasseb. According to Mohasseb, in the old days 'money was made easily and without any risk.' But 'it's different now with the inspectors and all the other dealers and the peasants who always want cash.' Having to evade the watchful eye of inspectors and deliver cash upfront to peasants who could not risk a second clandestine meeting raised the cost of doing business and ate into everyone's profits. But it also presented a very real danger to life and limb. Carrying so much cash over the unpoliced vastness of Egypt to the remote residences of poor antiquities hunters increased the chances of running into the omnipresent bandits that the country's political elites had failed to quell. Only by dressing as a woman and carrying his cash in a hidden money belt was Mohasseb able to transfer the wealth of Western and Egyptian elites into the hands of Egypt's poorest members of society.[21]

If anything, the activities of dealers in China were even more instructive than their counterparts in Egypt. This is because educated, wealthy Confucian gentlemen had been collecting the material remains of their own civilization for thousands of years without interruption. In other words, they did not need to wait until the arrival of Westerners in the modern era to start projecting a cultural or monetary value onto ancient works of art in East Asia. And yet, despite the fact that upper-class Chinese, Koreans and Japanese already cherished such things independently of Western customers, the end result was exactly the same as in Egypt, where virtually no one valued the monuments or artistic productions of pre-Islamic civilizations. That is to say, in East Asia as in Egypt, antiquities dealers facilitated a continuous flow of exquisite artwork to wealthy foreign customers whom they knew would transport such beloved purchases abroad, never to be seen again within their own countries. So why did they do it?

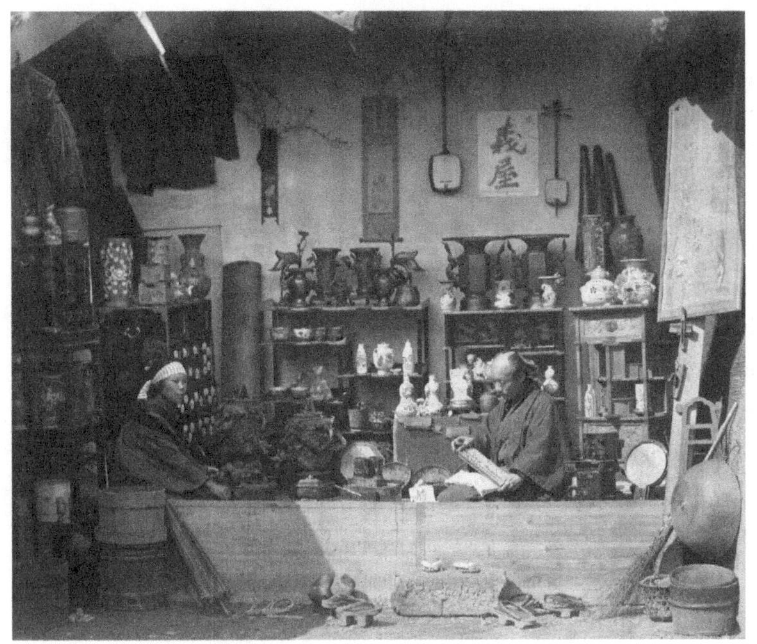

Antiquities shop in Japan, 1868, photograph by Felice Beato.

The answer is the same for dealers in China as it was in Egypt: no belief in a pre-existing 'nation' that owned everything under the soil and a firm conviction that anyone who already owned an old painting, vase or bronze had the inalienable right to dispose of it however they saw fit. A couple of examples of newly unearthed antiquities that changed hands several times before any Westerner ever got involved will help to illustrate this point. In the early eighteenth century, a bronze washbasin known as the Sanshipan was unearthed in the north-central province of Shaanxi. Because it had more than 350 ancient Chinese characters etched onto its surface, erudite Confucian scholars were able to determine that it was originally produced during the Western Zhou era – nearly 3,000 years ago. Such a valuable artefact would make for a great gift for anyone's boss. Not surprisingly, the first identifiable owner of the Sanshipan was Alinbao, the Qing viceroy of the region. He in turn regifted the Sanshipan to the Jiaqing Emperor for his fiftieth birthday in 1809. Thus we see the first enduring principle in action, wherein a treasure unloved by the earth is dug up by poor peasants and then used repeatedly to ingratiate its successive owners with the next person up on the hierarchy of imperial power.[22] This was a form of private gift-giving not dissimilar to that by which the Dunhuang manuscript examined in the previous chapter ended up – after numerous instances of regifting – in a mouldering trunk in Hawaii.

Another Chinese antiquity with a revealing history prior to the involvement of foreigners is the Maogongding, or '*ding* of the Duke of Mao'. This *ding*, or ancient bronze vessel, dated to the Western Zhou (1050–771 BC), was also found in Shaanxi, and also contained a rare inscription, this time totalling five hundred characters. Soon after its discovery in 1852, however, the Maogongding took a different path of transmission. Instead of circulating endlessly as a type of diplomatic gift, it first found its way into the hands of an antique dealer in Beijing 1,125 kilometres (700 mi.) away. From there it was shopped around to wealthy potential customers in the Qing imperial government to see who among them would be willing to pay top dollar. The winning bid was submitted by Chen Jieqi, who reportedly spent three years' worth of his salary to acquire it. Chen and his sons cherished it in private isolation for the next fifty years, until one of his heirs decided to sell it to the great Qing collector Duanfang in 1905 for a princely sum. When Duanfang was killed in the 1911 revolution, his wife turned it over to a bank in Tianjin as security for a mortgage. Once they paid back the mortgage, they briefly considered giving the Maogongding to one of their daughters as part of her dowry, but changed their minds and once again decided to use it as security

Rubbing of Maogongding, 1852.

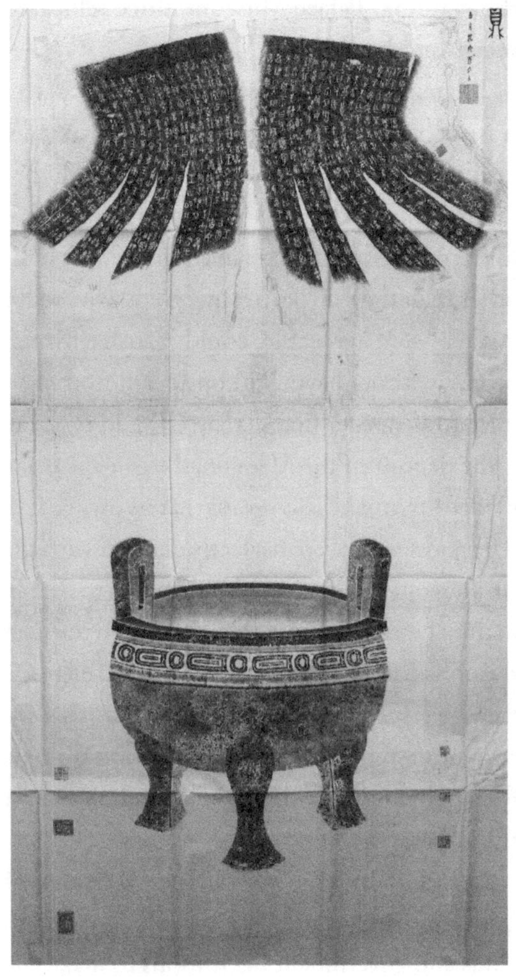

for another bank loan, this time to the Russian Daosheng Bank. From there it was purchased in 1926 by another wealthy Chinese businessman, Ye Gongchuo, whose family later sold it to an even wealthier Shanghai businessman a decade later. Finally, in 1947, long after new ideas about the 'Chinese nation' had been embraced by the ruling party, its last owner donated this well-travelled ancient bronze to the National Palace Museum, since relocated to Taipei, where it remains today.[23]

It is remarkable to note the many uses to which the Maogongding was put before it finally found its way into a museum: secluded admiration and analysis, an economic proxy for cash, security for a mortgage and even in consideration as part of a dowry. What all these forms of interaction have in common is that they concerned no one other than the two parties involved, who, so long as the terms of exchange were agreeable, could transfer ownership of this ancient bronze without having to consider any other competing claims. The means of transfer that perhaps should raise our eyebrows the most is the deposit of the Maogongding in a Russian-owned bank as the pledge for a loan. This means that its owner at the time – Duanfang's wife and sons – were perfectly content with the very real possibility that it would be confiscated and taken to Russia for sale on the international market should they default on the loan. But this was hardly the only instance of such behaviour. The late Qing court overseen by the powerful empress dowager, Cixi, and her successors after the 1911 revolution repeatedly offered treasures from the Forbidden City to foreign banks in Beijing as collateral for loans taken out to support the imperial household.[24]

In fact, in the days before cultural treasures became enshrined as 'priceless' emblems of modern nations, it was quite common for religious and government institutions to make ends meet by selling off things that would now be considered valuable heritage. In Japan during the 1870s, hundreds of struggling Buddhist monasteries sold some of their most valuable religious artwork to foreign collectors after the new Meiji government elevated Shinto to a state religion and withdrew previous subsidies for Buddhist institutions. In a period of just nine months in 1876–7, the French collector Émile Guimet

– founder of the Musée Guimet in Paris – managed to purchase more than three hundred religious paintings, six hundred statues and a thousand rare books and manuscripts from Japanese Buddhist monasteries and temples. In the 1920s, the stewards of the Xiuding Pagoda, located in the north-central Chinese province of Henan, sold off many of the exterior tiles of their sixth-century Buddhist pagoda, which made their way into a foreign museum. According to historian Nancy Steinhardt, this practice was 'not unique for Chinese religious architecture'.[25] In the 1930s, the monks who tended the Guangsheng Temple in Shanxi Province sold four large wall murals in order to raise funds to repair the roof of the main hall after it was damaged in an earthquake. Eventually, they were sold by a Chinese dealer to the Metropolitan Museum of Art in New York.[26]

Such practices seem shocking today, both in China and the West. But that is only because we have been conditioned to believe that everything in a museum represents the priceless heritage of some nation. In 2020 the Baltimore Museum of Art announced a plan to sell three paintings from its collection in order to raise up to $65 million for 'diversity and equity efforts'. Despite the politically correct cause, this bold proposal sparked a moral outcry from a range of critics who viewed it as a betrayal of the museum's mission. But it used to be quite common to treat art and antiquities in bald economic terms, so long as the return – stabilizing a family's finances, repairing a temple's roof – was deemed sufficient recompense *at the time* for the perceived value of what was sold. In 1917 a Chinese central government envoy named Xie Bin travelled to the northwestern province of Xinjiang, heard foreigners talking about the region's immaculately preserved mummies, and thought of a clever way to raise funds for the embattled provincial treasury. 'If only the state would issue a clear order stipulating their preservation,' he wrote, 'and then find a way to come up with the funds to ship and sell them abroad, the income generated by these mummies would be sufficient to supplement to some degree the financial situation of Xinjiang.'[27]

The history of antiquities dealers in China is so rich that any number of case studies could be examined to show just how welcoming the market was at the dawn of the twentieth century for the entry of big-pocketed Westerners. And because the antiquities trade flourished in China entirely independent of Western demand – unlike in Egypt – we do not need to rely upon the accounts of Western collectors to tell us how it operated. Many of the following case studies are drawn from the recollections of Chen Zhongyuan, a longtime Chinese participant within the domestic dealer market in Beijing and Shanghai during the 1930s and '40s. As an insider, Chen saw at first hand how Chinese art and antiquities made their way from rural

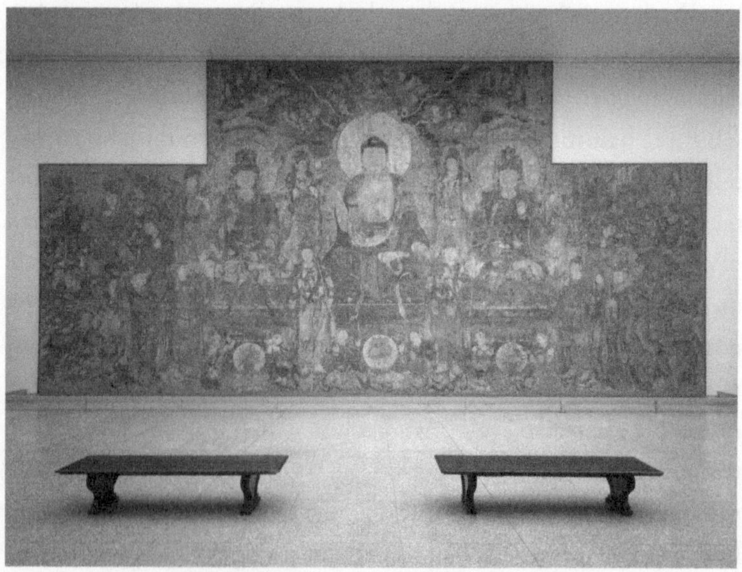

Wall murals from Guangsheng Temple at the Metropolitan Museum of Art, New York.

fields and private collections into urban antique shops, before finally ending up in the hands of Chinese, Japanese and Western customers. His personal recollections of early twentieth-century dealer networks in China provide an authentic and rare window into the means by which so many antiquities were taken abroad, without any of the cultural misunderstandings or mistranslations that occasionally mar the accounts of Western collectors.

In 1918 a peasant farmer in Zhengding County in Hebei Province, just south of Beijing, unearthed a gilded Buddhist statue and altarpiece while tilling his fields. Initially, he tried to keep the artefact for himself, most likely as a protective religious talisman, but his children blabbed about it to the neighbours and word quickly spread far and wide. Before long, someone from the local government office came knocking on his door. Back then, according to Chen, local government officials 'didn't concern themselves with anything peasants discovered, whoever found it, it belonged to them . . . They just wanted to take a look.' The local magistrate was impressed, saying that the discovery of a gilded buddha figurine from out of the blue was an auspicious sign of the Buddha manifesting himself in their county, and that its new peasant owner should take precautions to safeguard it.

Eventually, Chinese dealers in Beijing heard about the discovery and sent someone out to Zhengding County to try and purchase the statue and altarpiece. But its peasant owner refused to sell, on two grounds. First, he believed that it was solid gold rather than merely gilded bronze, which raised the asking price beyond what the dealer was willing to pay. And second, the statue was widely regarded within the county as an authentic spiritual manifestation of the Buddha, against which worldly cash could hardly compare – up to a point, that is. Once the Beijing dealers managed to inspect the figurine up close, they concluded that it was a Buddhist altarpiece (the Maitreya)

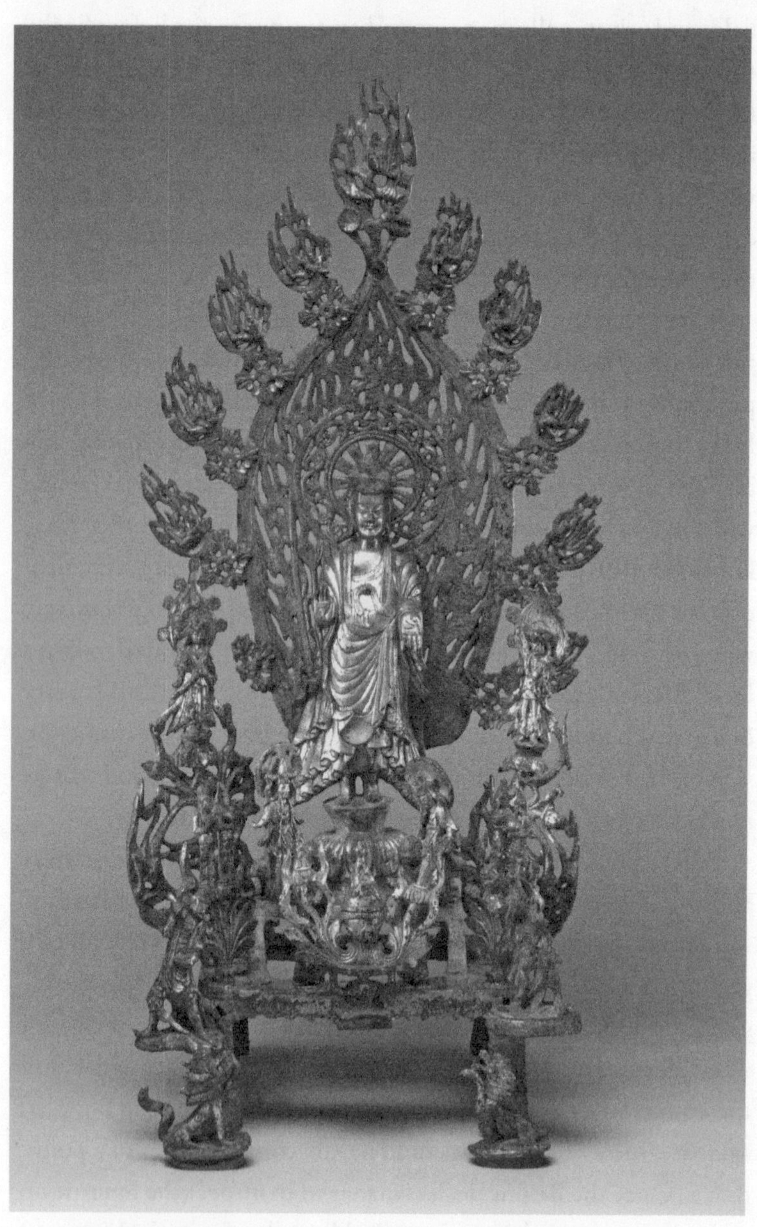

Buddha Maitreya altarpiece at the Metropolitan Museum of Art, New York.

that had been manufactured expressly for the emperor of the Northern Wei dynasty some 1,500 years ago; truly, a gift fit for a king. So three dealers decided to pool their resources together, wrote a letter to the local magistrate encouraging him to condone the sale as a means of raising money for their impoverished county, and tendered a handsome offer of 30,000 silver yuan. The offer was accepted, but the Maitreya's journey was far from over. The Beijing dealers soon sold it for an even greater profit to a Japanese dealer, who in turn took it to New York to find an even wealthier customer. That ended up being none other than Abby Rockefeller, the wife of Standard Oil heir John D. Rockefeller Jr, who paid $220,500 for the altarpiece (equivalent to roughly $4,779,400 today). In 1938 the Rockefellers sold it to the Metropolitan Museum of Art, where it remains to this day.[28]

All in all, this Buddhist altarpiece passed through four different hands in three different countries before it ended up inside a glass cabinet in the Met. Each time it changed hands, a clearly recognized owner was permitted to transfer his or her ownership of the altarpiece to anyone – Chinese, Japanese or American – who was willing to match its perceived valuation in cash. Of course, the factors that determined each valuation throughout the chain of supply were different for each transaction: the peasant demanded a price that matched his spiritual and economic assessment of the altarpiece, the Beijing dealers demanded a price that matched their expected profit margins in running an upscale business, and Abby Rockefeller demanded a price that matched her identity as a wealthy philanthropist and patron of the arts. No one begrudged the poor peasant discoverer his good luck in stumbling upon the altarpiece, since everyone knew that the earth did not love its treasures and finders keepers ruled the day. If the original peasant discoverer thought it was solid gold and represented the Buddha's favour, he was well within his rights not to sell it until a customer matched that valuation, however misguided it may have been. In the final analysis, all parties involved in these transactions respected the right of each subsequent owner to sell this Buddhist artefact to whomsoever they chose, whenever they chose and at whatever price they demanded.

Another story recollected by the dealer Chen involved the young wife of an older Chinese scholar who wanted to purchase a jade bracelet from an antique shop in Beijing. When the husband told his wife he couldn't afford it, she went behind his back and traded one of his most cherished antiquities to get it: an exquisite Northern Song inkwell fashioned from *jun*-ware, one of the rarest of ceramics. Not surprisingly, this led to severe marital tensions. The husband scolded his wife, telling her that the ceramic was a personal gift to him from the Guangxu Emperor during the late nineteenth century. As such, he considered it 'a family heirloom' worth more than a hundred of the jade bracelets she had exchanged it for. But his young wife defended her actions with a fascinating riposte. 'If Guangxu awarded it to you, then how could you go and kowtow in front of the Hongxian Emperor? Are these the actions of a loyal official?'[29] The 'Hongxian', or 'Great Constitution', emperor is a reference to Yuan Shikai, the military general who seized power after the 1911 revolution and four years later decided to resurrect the defunct monarchy under his own reign.

The wife's logic, according to the moral standards of her day, would have been widely embraced by most people in China. That is to say, her husband's ancient Song inkwell came into his possession as a symbol of the personal bond of loyalty that bound him to the monarch of one specific dynastic clan. So when he willingly chose to serve the self-appointed monarch of a second dynasty many years later, he effectively severed that first political bond, thereby undermining the original symbolic value of the antiquity that served as the physical embodiment of that bond. To the husband, this original political bond with the Guangxu Emperor conferred something close to a priceless value on the inkwell. But to his wife, her husband's subsequent betrayal of that political bond negated the moral basis of his priceless valuation, turning the inkwell into just another form of economic capital that she could use to purchase the jade bracelet that her stingy husband refused to buy for her.

It is important to note that neither the husband nor the wife regarded the inkwell as a symbol of the Chinese nation. Instead, the rhetorical contours of their marital spat revolved entirely around whether or not the personal bond between sovereign and subject had been severed, with major consequences for the market value of the antiquity that symbolized that bond. Once its contemporary valuation – according to contemporary moral standards, not the nationalist standards of our own day – was downgraded in the wife's eyes from priceless to precious, the inkwell quickly entered the international art market and was sold to a dealer in New York for a hefty profit. Its arrival in America symbolized not the betrayal or plunder of the Chinese nation, but rather the betrayal of one man's obligations of political loyalty to a long-dead emperor from a long-gone dynasty – and, of course, a dysfunctional marriage.

To most Chinese, selling art and antiquities to Western and Japanese collectors was just as natural as selling them to Chinese ones. Discrimination would be bad for business. The only difference was that Westerners took their purchases home to countries on the other side of the globe, and often later donated them to museums, never to be resold again. But such was the cost of doing business in an age when only the earth and individuals – not nations – could own art and antiquities. In the eyes of those who participated in the dealer supply chain in China, the unlikelihood of any artefact ever coming back to China once acquired by a Western collector was more than offset by the willingness of Westerners to overpay for things of dubious quality and authenticity. In fact, the recollections of the dealer Chen Zhongyuan make it clear that plenty of Chinese art made its way into Western museums simply because foreign customers were regarded as easy dupes who would pay an inflated price for inferior goods.

Two examples will suffice to show that sometimes artefacts ended up in the West not because Westerners were cunning, but because they were gullible. In 1930 a Song dynasty ceramic once gifted from the abdicated boy emperor Puyi to one of his Chinese teachers ended up in the storeroom of a Beijing antique dealer. The teacher's sons had sold it to make ends meet after their father died. The dealer began to despair that he had paid too high a price for a type of ceramic that was then out of fashion and would thus be unable to recoup his losses, much less turn a big profit. So another dealer advised him to 'go sell it to foreigners'. Once he played up its association with the last Qing emperor, some foreign buyer would 'definitely be willing to offer a high price for it'. Though in this particular case the first dealer concluded that foreign customers had also tired of this type of ceramic, the advice given by the second dealer suggests a deliberate strategy of targeting less knowledgeable Western buyers when Chinese buyers were in short supply.[30]

Another revealing anecdote concerns a debate between a pair of Chinese dealers from Shanghai and Beijing in 1941 over the authenticity of a plum blossom vase purported to be from the reign of the Ming emperor Yongle (1402–24). When Zheng Ruisheng, the Beijing dealer, learned of the assessment of the Shanghai dealer, Ye Shuchong, that the vase he had just bought for 5,000 yuan might be fake, he began to despair. 'Do you mean to tell me that this thing is a fake?' Ye calmed his colleague down by reminding him that less discerning Americans might still pay a high price for it, and that both of them could benefit from their gullibility:

> I'm telling you it's disputed, not that it's definitely a fake. If I really thought it was a fake, I wouldn't have come. I want to discuss with you the idea of sending it to America. Here in China some people say it's from the Yongle era, others say it isn't, and we'll just debate it endlessly with no result. But in New York, if [the Chinese dealer] C. T. Loo says it is Yongle, what foreigner is going to dispute that?

Faced with such irrefutable logic, Zheng agreed to work with Ye to export the vase to New York and sell it to a wealthy American buyer. Unfortunately for Zheng, the Japanese attack on Pearl Harbor later that year cut off transport links across the Pacific, and the vase remained in China by chance rather than by intent.[31]

The irresistible pull of a big American payday is a constant theme throughout Chen's recollections of the dealer network in China. Record-breaking sales to prominent museums in New York, Boston and Washington, DC, were a mark of pride for Chinese dealers, who openly bragged about such transactions as a badge of honour. And why shouldn't they brag about their impressive business acumen? All of them grew up in a world in which the appreciation of art knew no borders, Western interest in Chinese culture was flattering and lucrative, and no one owned anything other than what they personally found, bought, inherited or commissioned. But sometimes the desire to cash in on wealthy or naive American customers could lead to unhappy endings. This was the case with the so-called Chu Silk Manuscript, which was unearthed in 1942 from a Warring

States tomb by Chinese subsistence diggers in the southern city of Changsha.

This ancient silk manuscript, which appears to record ancient zodiac and other astrological data through the depiction of twelve charming monsters spaced around its margins, was sold, in predictable fashion, by the 'tomb raiders' to an urban dealer in Changsha. From there it was bought again by a local antiquities dealer and amateur historian named Cai Jixiang. He kept it hidden throughout years of warfare and strife with Japan, until finally making his way to Shanghai in 1946. There he contracted the services of Ye Shuchong, the same dealer who advised his colleagues in Beijing to make a financial killing off rich Americans rather than deal with picky Chinese customers. With Ye's backing, Cai got in touch with one of his old American acquaintances, John Hadley Cox, then working for the Office of Strategic Services. Surviving letters between the two reveal that Cai gave the Chu Silk Manuscript to Cox in the hope of selling it in America. Cox paid Cai $1,000 up front, with the promise of an additional $9,000 once he sold the manuscript abroad. Of course, Cai could have just as easily sold the Chu Silk Manuscript to a Chinese dealer or to any other wealthy customer. But the allure of a massive American payday proved too enticing to pass up, and Cox took the manuscript abroad to earn his commission. But, contrary to all expectations, Cox was unable to find a buyer, and Cai, apparently disheartened, wrote to Cox asking him to send the manuscript back, promising to return the initial $1,000 down payment. Cox never wrote back, and the Communist takeover of China in 1949 made it impossible for any further communication between the two men.

Eventually, Cox sold the manuscript in 1965 along with another part of his collection to a Chinese American dealer who was acting on behalf of the pharmaceutical magnate Arthur M. Sackler. Sackler, who is believed to have paid somewhere in the region of $500,000 for the manuscript, then donated it to the Freer and Sackler Museum in Washington, DC, where it remains to this day.[32] Some Chinese and Western scholars have called for its return to China, characterizing its loss as yet another instance of plundered loot taken from China by foreign imperialists. It might be more instructive to think of the Chu Silk Manuscript as one of the rare instances of seller's remorse on the part of Chinese dealers who willingly and knowingly attempted to squeeze a bigger payday out of their cultural inventory. In other words, Cai Jixiang did not ask Cox to send this precious manuscript back to China because he regretted his role in depriving China of its supposedly inalienable cultural treasures. He asked for its return because he and Ye Shuchong did not receive their anticipated share of the eye-popping American sums that all parties believed could be fetched across the Pacific.

Surviving letters show that if Cox had actually returned the manuscript to China, Cai had plans to sell it to another buyer immediately. In the end, this was a business deal gone bad between two men who wanted to get rich quick by following the time-honoured tradition of selling privately owned or earth-relinquished goods to the customer with the biggest wallet – wherever in the world he or she might be found. There were other potential customers in China that Cai could have sold to, but he chose instead to target the most lucrative market he could find, one with both the biggest potential payoff and the biggest potential risk. Simply put, Cai and Ye got burned; the Chinese nation did not get plundered. And perhaps most importantly for the historian who wishes to treat history like a will, this is precisely how Cai interpreted his loss at the time – as a personal financial setback. It was only three decades later, under the intense ideological fervour of the Cultural Revolution, that he began to reinterpret his sour memories of this transaction by reframing the whole episode as an instance of the Chinese nation being taken advantage of by unscrupulous foreign imperialists.[33]

In terms of the sheer volume of Chinese antiquities that were exported out of China during the first half of the twentieth century, no dealer can compare to Lu Qinzhai, who is better known in English as C. T. Loo. Loo's career as a dealer spanned some four decades until the Communist takeover in 1949, and he was responsible for some of the most spectacular showpieces that grace the Asian art collections of major American museums today. Born in 1880 to a poor and

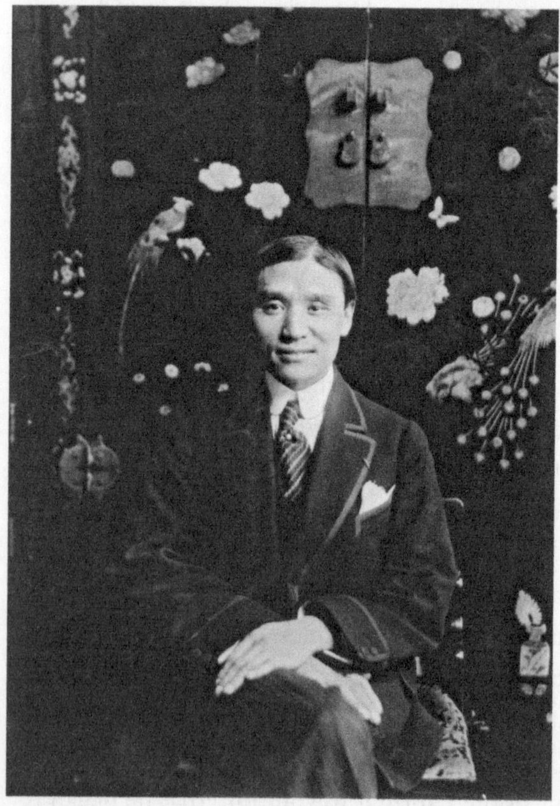

Chinese dealer C. T. Loo, 1910s.

undistinguished rural family in the southeastern province of Zhejiang, Loo left home as a young boy and found work as a servant in the household of the much wealthier and scholarly Zhang clan in the city of Nanxun. Loo started out as a cook, before being assigned to Zhang Jingjiang, the patriarch's second son. In 1902 Zhang's father, alarmed by his son's growing revolutionary fervour, shipped him off to Paris to take up a minor diplomatic post in the Qing Embassy. Loo, now 22 years old, went with him.[34]

Nothing speaks to Loo's future career as the world's foremost dealer of Chinese art better than his first assignment upon arrival in Paris: helping Zhang Jingjiang run a successful export business. Zhang wasted little time in forming the Tongyun Company. Its motto? 'Prosperous business across the four seas, lavish fortunes along the three rivers.' Zhang started out selling Chinese silk, tea leaves, rugs, ceramics and lacquerware, with various antiques supplied by his uncle back in China. Loo's job was to pick up the incoming goods at customs, fill out the paperwork, and then stock the shop and sell Zhang's wares to French and Chinese customers in Paris. It was perfect on-the-job training for a future dealer: all Loo needed to do was learn how to swap silk and tea for paintings and bronzes.

By 1908, after several years of handsome profits, Zhang packed up his bags and returned to China. He soon became involved with revolutionary activities against the ruling dynasty, then rose to great heights within Chiang Kai-shek's Nationalist Party after it seized power in the late 1920s. But while Zhang's head was awash with newfangled ideas about saving 'the Chinese nation', Loo remained behind in Paris and continued to adhere to the businessman's ethos of treating all people, from all nations, as potential sources of profit. He started his own business, Laiyuan ('goods from afar'), shifted his focus almost entirely to Chinese art and antiquities, and began making annual summer trips back to China via the Trans-Siberian Railroad to meet with dealers in Beijing and Shanghai (Ye Shuchong became Loo's preferred Shanghai liaison). Each time he returned to China, Loo would leave behind photographs of the sorts of items that his European and American customers desired. For example, one photograph found in his archives after his death contained the following handwritten caption: 'You can look for this kind of Buddha's head.'

Loo did not create the domestic dealer market within China, nor was he the first Chinese dealer to sell to foreigners. His great innovation was to extend the supply chain of Chinese antiquities all the way from the abandoned rural tombs of China across the world directly to the downtown shopping areas of major Western cities. In other words, once Loo opened up shops in Paris, London and New York, rich Westerners who wanted to buy Chinese art no longer had to travel to China – Loo brought Chinese art to them. And one of the few things Western collectors valued that Chinese collectors did not value was popular religious art. The caption about a 'Buddha's head' on one of Loo's photographs speaks precisely to this sense of disconnect. To the cultured Confucian gentleman in China, popular religious art – Buddhist and Daoist statues and figurines, stone reliefs of deities, and ritual implements – were little more than superstitious baubles blindly worshipped by the ignorant masses. They were not fit for the serious attentions of wealthy men who prided themselves on their education. In 1928 the Chinese archaeologist Huang Wenbi bemoaned this cultural blind spot of his peers. 'People in our country are accustomed to emphasizing research on the upper classes and ignoring the lower classes,' he wrote.[35]

To Loo, however, this blind spot opened up a very tempting opportunity. If Chinese customers were unwilling to pay top dollar for popular religious art – or any dollar at all – what was stopping him from selling such things to Western customers who would? We have already seen the tendency of impoverished Buddhist monasteries to sell parts of their collections in order to raise funds for renovations. But China was also filled with plenty of open-air religious sites located in close proximity to destitute rural communities. One of the most famous and impressive of these is the Longmen Grottoes near the ancient capital of Luoyang in the north-central plains. Consisting of 2,345 caves carved out of a cliff alongside the picturesque Luo River, Longmen was once home to as many as 100,000 sculptured images and nearly 2,500 steles. Who owned all of these statues and bas-reliefs, which were carved out of the rock over a thousand years ago by anonymous craftsmen? There seemed to be no clear answer. What was clear, however, was that once it became known that wealthy Western clients would pay considerable sums of money for this sort of fine Buddhist sculpture, the statues of Longmen began to disappear. Today, it is estimated that about 85 per cent of all the Buddhist statuary once extant at Longmen is no longer attached to the walls of its original grotto.[36]

C. T. Loo, as the final node in the international dealer supply chain, played an integral part in stimulating demand for this sort of vulnerable popular religious art, which can be found in many Western museums and private collections today. How do we pass judgement on what happened at Longmen in the early twentieth century? It is easy to blame the agents of Western museums for stimulating nearly all of the demand for these depredations by paying large sums of money for the pieces that showed up in antique shops in Beijing and Shanghai. After all, few Chinese were buying them, for they had inherited a strong cultural bias against collecting popular religious art – so Westerners (and Japanese) were the only major customers. Several of

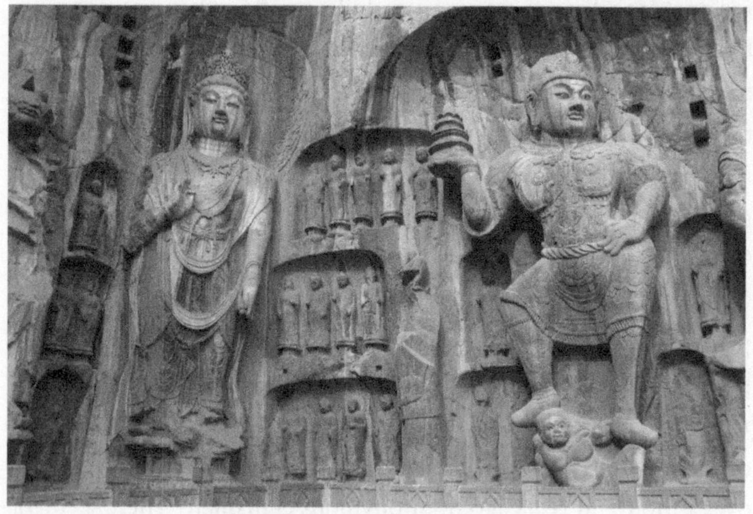

Longmen Grottoes, Luoyang, China.

the Americans who bought fragments from Longmen and other public religious sites seem to have anticipated future critiques, since they took the trouble of publicly defending their actions as an act of preservation during a time when Chinese authorities could not protect these artefacts and Chinese scholars were not yet interested in studying them.

And yet we cannot blame just the foreigners alone. After all, in most cases they didn't physically remove the statues and reliefs with their own hands; they simply provided the economic motivation for someone like Loo to circulate photographs of popular religious art with an encouragement for others to look for these kinds of artefacts. Loo, of course, was Chinese, as was his agent in Shanghai. But they didn't chip the statues away from the cave surface, either. So who did? We have only incomplete and woefully inadequate descriptions of how the subsistence digger supply chain operated before objects were delivered to the antique shop itself. In 1914 an editorial in *The Times*

(London) criticized the removal of public religious art in China, claiming that statues that appeared on the market were 'mangled, sawn asunder or broken into pieces by clumsy thieves, in order that fragments may be taken to Peking and sold to European dealers'.[37]

This cursory reference to 'clumsy thieves' is vague and imprecise: who exactly were they? Local villagers? Bandits? In 1944 the American curator Alan Priest provided a slightly more specific account: 'the little village near Lung Men stands watch, but from across the river men waded armpit-deep and chipped fragments from the surface at night. These they took down to Chengchow, where agents of the Peking dealers bought them.' If true, then this version of events suggests that those who physically removed the sculptures were not locals, since they had to wade across the river and do their work at night, all while the closest village 'stands watch'. Though more detailed, this description still contains gaps in logic: if the residents of the closest village disapproved of all these removals to the point where they were determined to 'stand watch', then how could they nonetheless allow 85 per cent of all Buddhist statuary to be taken away over a period of several decades, when it was clear that the 'thieves' came by night and had to cross a treacherous river to get there? In 2007 a Chinese television documentary claimed that a dealer named Yue Bin commissioned a 'scoundrel' in Luoyang to provide a series of stone heads. This 'scoundrel' then turned to a 'group of bandits . . . near Longmen to browbeat their own village's three stone cutters to hammer the frieze' off its grotto wall.[38] But the documentary provides no historical sources for these claims.

All this analysis may seem like little more than splitting hairs to many readers. After all, the objects ended up on display in Western museums, with the final point of sale pointing squarely to Loo or one of his colleagues. So surely Western customers and Chinese traitors can shoulder all the blame. And yet the details matter. In Egypt, we have already witnessed the class-based origins of pejorative terms such as 'tomb robber', 'illicit digger' and 'bandits'. More often than not, these terms are deployed by wealthy educated elites to delegitimize the activities of their lower-class competitors and criminalize their poverty. But 'scoundrels' and 'bandits' are usually synonymous with 'subsistence diggers'. And those who may appear as bandits to privileged outsiders can just as frequently turn out to be embraced by the communities who shelter them in exchange for the security and protection that their own national governments do not provide. Virtually no serious research exists on what illiterate peasants living in the vicinity of 'plundered' cultural sites throughout history actually thought about this 'plunder', or whether they themselves even participated in it.

Such questions matter, however, because they carry enormous implications for the attribution of moral responsibility in our own day for this historical desecration of public religious art. If the domestic dealers in Loo's supply chain really did hire lawless bandits who then proceeded to terrorize helpless villagers into reluctantly peeling away the objects of their religious devotion, then both Loo and his customers in Western museums seem to deserve the lion's share of the blame, thus bolstering calls for the return of these museum artefacts. But it is not at all clear that this was the case, despite the hasty proclamations of moral entrepreneurs today. On the contrary, a preponderance of evidence points to the active and enthusiastic participation of poor peasants in the removal of cultural antiquities from their midst in exchange for various forms of economic compensation.

Was this participation the same for both an ancient Confucian stele whose inscription they could not read as it was for an actively worshipped bodhisattva statue whose spiritual consent was viewed as indispensable for bringing rain to fields stricken by drought? We simply do not know. But it does not seem unreasonable to conclude that, much like those Easter Islanders who willingly gifted away spiritually diminished moai statues, poor peasants in early twentieth-century China may have taken their miserable fates as evidence that the gods had either forsaken them or had lost their divine powers entirely. If so, then they could hardly be blamed for exchanging the material manifestations of these gods for ready cash that could feed their family for another day. In our examination of the dealer network in Egypt we did not have to confront such thorny issues, for few people other than Western-educated elites identified in any meaningful way with the pharaonic gods.

But it matters greatly in the case of China. If the peasants who chiselled away the Longmen sculptures were Chinese, if the villagers tasked with guarding the grottoes were Chinese, if the local strongmen (if such they were) who directed them from Luoyang were Chinese, if the agents of the dealers who commissioned the Luoyang strongmen were Chinese, if the governor of Shaanxi Province was Chinese, if all the staff on the train from Luoyang to Shanghai were Chinese, if Loo's colleague in Shanghai was Chinese, if the customs agents who inspected these antiquities for export were Chinese, if Loo himself was Chinese, and if no firearms or coercive force of any sort were involved in this extensive chain of supply across the globe, then who shall we blame for the so-called plunder of China? In addition to a handful of Americans who wrote a cheque payable to C. T. Loo, is the entire Chinese population complicit in the theft of its own national heritage? At what point must we conclude that nearly everyone – with the sole exception of today's armchair moral entrepreneurs, of course – was either an imperialist thief or a nationalist traitor?

The widespread and enthusiastic complicity of Chinese facilitators throughout government and society is nowhere more evident than in the fate of a new law passed by the Republican government just a few years after the fall of the last imperial dynasty. In 1914 President Yuan Shikai issued an order prohibiting the export of antiquities from China.[39] But even the president's own family did not enforce the law. Take, for example, the fate of six stone reliefs that depicted the favourite steeds of Emperor Taizong (r. 598–649) of the Tang dynasty. For well over a thousand years, they graced a corridor known as a 'spirit path' at the royal Tang mausoleum of Zhaoling, not far from Luoyang. Western admirers sometimes referred to them as China's version of the Elgin Marbles. In 1913 a French dealer commissioned the removal of two of the reliefs, but 'the men transporting them were attacked by peasants and the precious relics

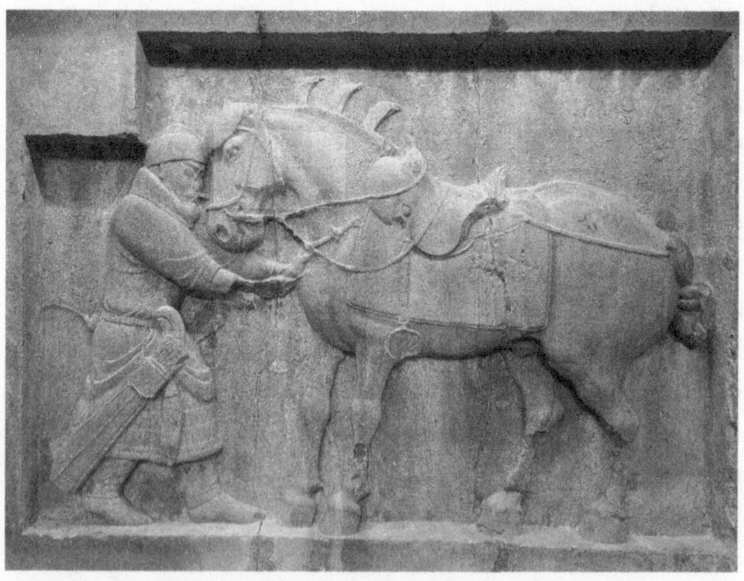

Emperor Taizong horse relief, *c.* 636–49,
one of the Six Steeds of Zhao Mausoleum.

thrown down a precipice.'[40] Here we have an unambiguous display of local animosity towards the attempted removal of a cultural artefact to a Western collector; had these men managed to successfully remove these reliefs in spite of this peasant attack, the case for their return today would be compelling and strong.

Unfortunately, the story of their removal does not end with this rousing display of local resistance. The two reliefs, once recovered, were not returned to their original location or placed within any site of potential safekeeping. Instead, they were given – by whom is not clear – to the local provincial military commander in order to win his favour. He in turn gave them to President Yuan Shikai, who appears to have intended to use them as ceremonial display pieces in Beijing to bolster his ill-fated restoration of the monarchy in 1915. All of these exchanges constitute textbook cases of art and antiquities being used as a form of diplomatic capital among Chinese officials. After Yuan died in 1916 with his family in political disgrace, one of his sons apparently sold the two stone reliefs to a Chinese dealer named Zhao Hefang, who in turn sold them to C. T. Loo. Loo then sold them to the University of Pennsylvania Museum. Much later, when these horses became abstract symbols of China's national humiliation, Loo defended his actions with pointed words: 'If a thing bought through the President, was not legal, [then] who would have the authority to sell? And if it was legal at that time but no more legal now, then how many dealers and collectors would be in the same situation?'[41]

Loo's comment, while self-serving, should still give us pause. Indeed, how should the historian pass judgement on laws that almost no one observed, including the president himself? Today, the constitution of the People's Republic of China guarantees both freedom of speech and assembly. As human rights advocates would argue, however, these laws are hardly worth the paper they are printed on.

The 1914 antiquities export prohibition law was the same. For at least a decade after the fall of the Qing dynasty in 1911, newly unemployed imperial officials and their families sold off large portions of their art collections in order to make ends meet. The most famous instance was the sale of Duanfang's magnificent collection to the Metropolitan Museum of Art. This deal was brokered by John C. Ferguson, a Canadian missionary turned foreign advisor to the new Republican government. 'The family', Ferguson wrote in 1914, 'has been left with not much else than the art specimens which the father collected during his life.' As a result, 'it has nearly driven me to bankruptcy to try to buy as much as I have.' Stories like this were legion – and most of them took place well after passage of the 1914 law.[42]

If there was any doubt about the illegitimacy of the new antiquities export prohibition law among most Chinese officials, those doubts were firmly put to rest during an exhibition of Chinese treasures in London two decades later. In 1935 Chiang Kai-shek signed off on the shipment of 735 exquisite works of art and antiquities to be sent to the Royal Academy of Arts for inclusion in a rare display of China's art. Designed in part to drum up support for Chiang's government among powerful Western powers in its struggle against the Japanese military, this exhibition also included a towering 6-metre-tall (20 ft) marble statue of the Amitabha Buddha that Loo had acquired from a temple in Hebei Province, but for which he had been unable to find a buyer. So he recouped his financial losses by turning the statue into a form of advertising for his business. The deal he brokered with Nationalist officials was as follows: in exchange for insisting that the British curators add Loo's name to the official display placard, Loo would donate the statue to the Chinese government, which would in turn donate it to the British Museum as a symbol of goodwill between the two countries.

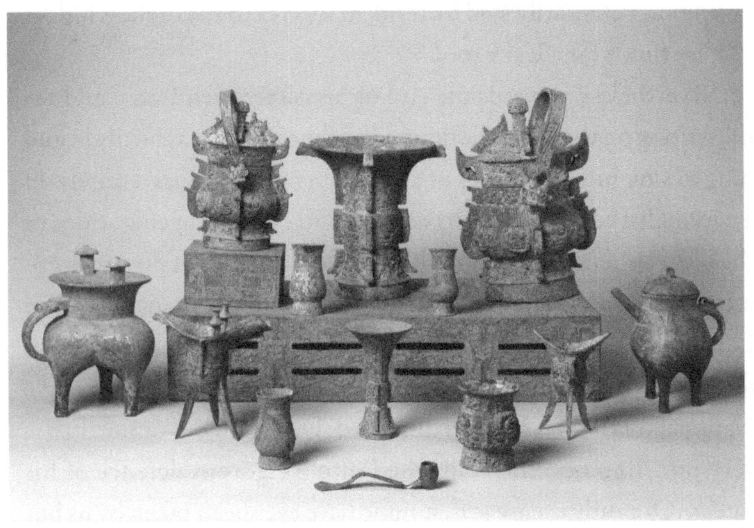

Duanfang's collection of ancient bronzes sold to the Metropolitan Museum of Art, New York.

Loo's name remains on the placard today, and all parties involved got what they wanted: the British Museum got a towering showcase Buddhist statue, the Chinese government got diplomatic capital from Great Britain and Loo's business got free advertising for as long as the statue remains on display. Thus not only did Chiang Kai-shek's own government officials willingly and enthusiastically cooperate with a known 'thief' like Loo, they also went out of their way to place the central government's own stamp of approval on the same art dealership that was responsible for so many transgressions of the virtually meaningless antiquities export prohibition law. After the war, Chiang Kai-shek even went so far as to confer upon Loo a medal for his help with the London exhibition and wartime charity efforts. Apparently, no one in the Chinese government ever bothered to make enquiries into just how Loo got this statue from that Hebei temple in the first place. If past precedent is any guide, it was in all likelihood voluntarily sold by resident monks to the highest bidder to raise funds for a leaky roof.[43]

Nevertheless, towards the end of his career even Loo could see the writing on the wall. The discourse of the nation was finally beginning to sink into the minds of a new generation weaned entirely on a nationalist educational curriculum. And once the ageing scions of the older generation – who believed in the sanctity of private property and finders keepers – began to die off, cosmopolitan dealers like Loo scrambled to defend their past actions. In 1940 Loo claimed to feel 'so ashamed to have been one of the sources by which these National treasures have been dispersed'. Disingenuous or not, in the very next line Loo then launched into a vigorous defence of his career. 'Our only excuse is that none have ever been taken by us but all bought in the open market in competition with other buyers.' He then continued: 'as Art has no frontiers, these sculptures going forth into the world, admired by scholars as well as the public, may do more good for China than any living Ambassador.' The public display of the treasures he sold to Western museums, he argued, 'make the world realize our ancient civilization and culture thus serving to create a love and better understanding of China and the Chinese people'.[44] Having grown up in a world where people of all economic and political backgrounds within China – from the president on high to the peasants down low – routinely treated art and antiquities as alienable commodities, it seems unlikely that Loo went to his grave with any true feelings of remorse or regret.

Let us conclude our analysis of dealers with one of the most memorable recollections of Chen Zhongyuan, the venerable Chinese dealer. In 1996 Chen recalled the incredible journey of a rare Song dynasty vase of the distinct ceramic ware known as *ge*. In 1860, during the British plunder and burning of the Old Summer Palace, a drunk 'foreign devil' soldier threw something onto a street in Beijing. An old Chinese man walked over to pick it up, thought it might be some sort of antique and sold it to the first dealer he could find. It turned out to be a flawless example of Song *ge*-ware, something only an emperor could have owned. Over the next seven decades, it passed through three generations of the dealer's family (one of whom used it as a common flower vase in his home) before finally being sold off twice more to various Chinese dealers. About 1932 or so, the last Chinese dealer to own it sold it to the British Museum for £10,000.[45]

The response of Chen's dealer friend Xiao Shunong? 'Can you believe it? Seventy-two years ago a British soldier didn't take it away as plunder, and yet it still ends up in the hands of the British!' In other words, when faced with an agent of Western imperialism who actually attempted to give back what he had taken, the Chinese treated the ceramic not as a priceless symbol of their nation to be preserved for posterity, but rather as a privately owned bauble that would eventually be sold back, with great enthusiasm, to those same Western 'imperialists' at a substantial profit, thus completing a transfer of wealth from the emperor to the descendants of his lowliest of subjects.

C. T. Loo would have been proud.

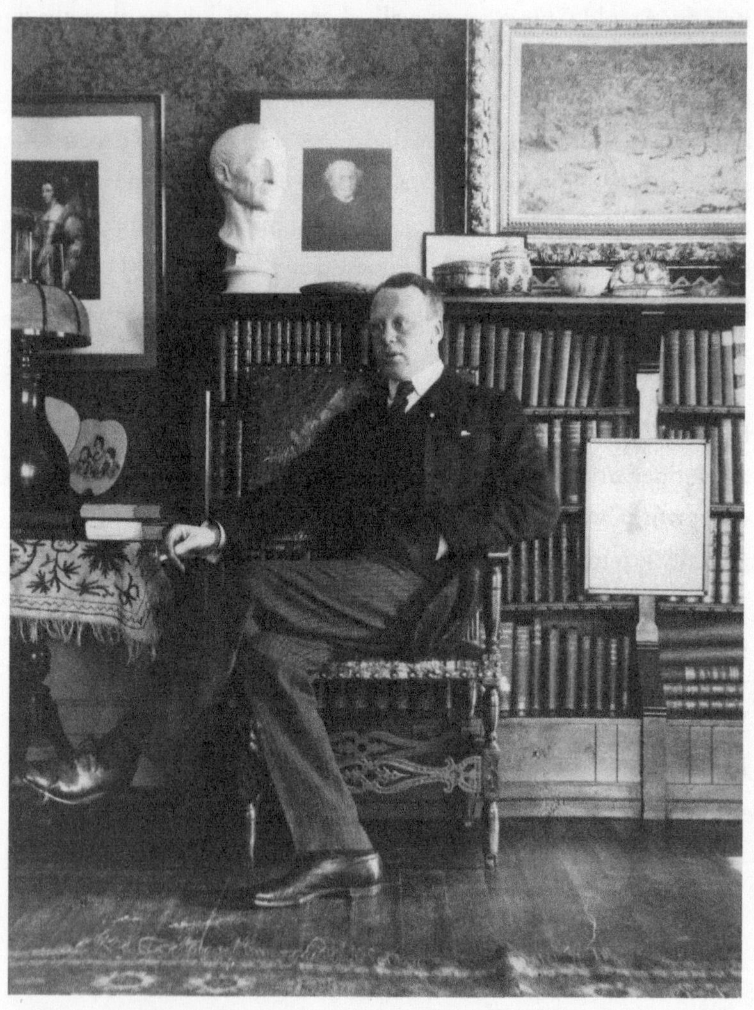

Harvard art historian Langdon Warner, *c.* 1910–16.

3

EXCAVATIONS AND EXPEDITIONS

What was the difference between an archaeologist and a dealer? To help us further distinguish between the two, let us take a closer look at a pair of reactions that Gilded Age magnates Charles Lang Freer and John D. Rockefeller Jr had in their dealings with two different types of collectors. In 1907 Freer undertook a trip to Asia, where he intended to purchase art and antiquities for his growing private collection. While visiting a temple, he discovered that the attending priests were in fact Japanese dealers in disguise, who were trying to solicit a higher asking price for their wares by disguising them in a more authentic religious setting. 'The story is an amazing one,' he later wrote, 'particularly the part played by dealers, long enough for a sensational novel, unholy enough to satisfy a missionaries' [*sic*] dream and beset with the greatest aesthetic pitfalls I have thus far met.'[1]

In order to safeguard against the odious reputation of some of his colleagues, the prominent Chinese dealer C. T. Loo kept a long list of scholarly references to hand out to potential clients unfamiliar with his business.[2] This was a prudent move on his part, since several of Loo's most wealthy customers had occasion at one time or another to doubt the fairness of his dealings with them. Actual scholars, however, had no such need of reference lists. In 1922 the

Harvard art historian Langdon Warner submitted an application for funding to John D. Rockefeller Jr for an expedition to China. Warner's failure to give any details regarding the final intended destination of the art and antiquities he expected to acquire did not faze Rockefeller in the least. 'It is not clear from your letter what disposition is to be made of such treasures and material,' wrote Rockefeller's secretary, 'but Mr Rockefeller assumes Harvard University is to have whatever is found.'[3]

In other words, an archaeologist's employer instantly vouched for his credibility: to Rockefeller, anyone affiliated with an august institution of learning such as Harvard could only be a true scholar with the most impeccable intentions. But a dealer was a freelance businessman, not a tenured professor. Loo catered to the vain pretensions of a wealthy clientele by selling them the material trappings of upper-class gentility and cultural respectability, all while turning a handsome profit. By contrast, Warner professed adherence to the supposedly altruistic and politically disinterested ideals of scientific enquiry, all while subsisting on a modest, fixed salary. As a result, when asking for large sums of money from the wealthiest people on the planet, scholars were given the benefit of the doubt while dealers were not.

Of course, scholars like Warner did not always deserve the benefit of the doubt. During his subsequent expedition to northwest China in 1924, Warner boldly cut out several portions of ancient murals from the Buddhist grottoes at Dunhuang, an act of vandalism that elicited vociferous opposition from the poor peasants who still worshipped the gods depicted in these caves. Two decades earlier, the German archaeologist Albert von Le Coq brazenly cut out another set of Buddhist murals in the grottoes of Ming-oi, leaving garish saw marks in his wake. Though the local Muslim peasants who lived near this site expressed utter indifference to Le Coq's butchery of long-dead Buddhist gods, other European scholars were outraged. In 1907 the archaeologist Aurel Stein described Le Coq's excavation methods as a 'system for which the German language supplies the express term of "Rabbau" [robber]'. The Russian explorer Sergey Oldenburg characterized it as 'sheer robbery, clever, ingenious, but robbery all the same – not scholarly research'.[4]

Nevertheless, among the four different types of collectors under scrutiny in this book – diplomats, soldiers, dealers and scholars – scholars consistently came closer than any other group to living up to the Enlightenment ideals of science, preservation and education. And evidence of their commitment to these ideals was enshrined in their association with public institutions of higher learning. In other words, it was simply assumed that any artefact they uncovered would eventually be deposited into a museum, library or university. Of course, dealers also frequently deposited their goods into museums – but only if the museum happened to be the highest bidder. If not, incomparable works of art were just as likely to end up adorning the billiards hall of a private mansion, where they would be subjected to the destructive whims of their eccentric private owners. In her insightful study of private collectors throughout history, Erin L. Thompson has revealed the many idiosyncratic interactions that wealthy owners often had with their jealously hoarded artistic possessions, including the castration of an ancient statue of the Greek god Hermaphroditus and collectors who kissed and embraced their stone figurines when no one was looking. In China, it was common for Confucian collectors to cut up ancient manuscripts and hand out the pieces to friends and colleagues as gifts.[5]

So while not everything found in a museum today was put there by scholars, nearly everything that a scholar found was indeed put into a museum or other institution of higher learning. For our purposes here, the word 'scholar' is an umbrella term that includes a range of highly specialized applications: Egyptologist, archaeologist, Indologist, philologist, sinologist, ethnologist, anthropologist, historian and so on. When acting in an official scholarly capacity, their means of collecting tended to be expressed in one of two modes: stationary excavations and mobile expeditions. In most areas of concern to us, the distinction between excavations and expeditions is merely academic, with expeditions simply consisting of repeated excavations over the course of a continuous journey across great distances for many months or years at a time. The only significant variations between the two concern the greater logistical difficulties and dangers of an expedition, along with the perceptions of people in the host country towards such a risky undertaking, perceptions that usually tilted to the scholar's advantage.

Unlike all other means of antiquity removal, scholars engaged in excavations and expeditions tended to be drowning in bureaucratic paperwork. Dealers talked little about the internal mechanisms of their trade, soldiers let their guns do the talking and diplomats relied on informal relationships that frequently lacked precise written documentation. But scholars, who tended to come from modest economic backgrounds, had to uphold the scientific credibility and altruistic pretensions of their institutional sponsors if they wanted to receive funding for their next venture. This gave them a vested interest in obtaining the consent of all possible stakeholders in those countries where their archaeological operations were to be carried out: central government officials, local officials, the poor peasants whom they intended to hire for manual labour, and rival Western scholars, whose scientific approval of their excavation methods was deemed essential. If any of these groups found reason to complain about the actions of the scholar during the course of his excavation or expedition, he risked embarrassment for his host institution back home and the subsequent loss of future funding opportunities for himself.

This was a difficult juggling act. Nevertheless, it was one that incentivized the scholar to adopt a conservative approach to his work. Diplomats could rely on political favours, soldiers on brute force and dealers on cash. But the scholar had to rely on universal consensus, for he was the most vulnerable of all Western collectors. Too many people had the ability to sabotage his entire scholarly undertaking simply by saying no. To a lesser extent this was true of all Western collectors other than the soldier, but it was even more so with the scholar. Thus we often have a wealth of documentation for excavations and expeditions carried out by scholars: passports, funding applications, field diaries, letters, photographs and account books. And those are just the documents that one can find in the archives. Scholars were also expected to publish detailed scientific accounts of their discoveries for other scholars, while some even authored popular accounts for a general audience eager to experience vicariously the thrills of the expedition trail.

All this is to say that scholars were the least likely of all Western collectors to transgress the moral boundaries of their own day and age. After all, their professional survival depended on it. Few things they did were carried out in secret, and nearly everyone in any given locale was, by necessity, privy to their activities – many were a direct participant in them. Conversely, when the intellectual climate in non-Western host countries evolved to the point where Western scholars were no longer welcome, it turned out to be surprisingly easy to obstruct them. To this day, diplomats, soldiers and dealers continue to transport antiquities around the world through various informal conduits, sometimes necessitating the suspension, evasion or even revision of long-standing laws in order to do so. But excavations and expeditions conceived and implemented almost entirely by Western scholars have a very clear end point in most parts of the world. This is because Western scholars were so very vulnerable – and thus so very easy to stop once new political conditions warranted their expulsion from the host country. The fact that they were so easy to stop at the end of their era, however, should also serve as a reminder of the high degree of consensus that they were able to obtain during the heyday of their era, for it would have been a simple matter to obstruct them had anyone in the host country been inclined to do so.

The first stationary excavations whose organizers aspired to any sort of scientific standard were those carried out by the Swiss-German military engineer Karl Jakob Weber at the ancient Roman sites of Herculaneum and Pompeii in the middle of the eighteenth century. In 1750 Weber was appointed by the Spanish Bourbon king of Naples and Sicily to take over the reins from his predecessor, a man named Roque Joaquín de Alcubierre, who began digging tunnels into the subterranean site of Herculaneum in 1738. For over a decade, Alcubierre had treated Herculaneum as little more than an antiquarian quarry, from whence he could recover unique Roman sculptures and mosaics to decorate the king's new Portici Palace a few kilometres away. In order to ensure that only his king had access to such incomparable treasures, Alcubierre ordered the vandalism of murals his workmen were unable to take away, the smashing of duplicate statues and the refilling of all tunnels once easily accessible portable antiquities had been removed or destroyed.

Weber tried to change all that. Instead of viewing Herculaneum as a cultural mine, he floated the novel idea of preserving excavated

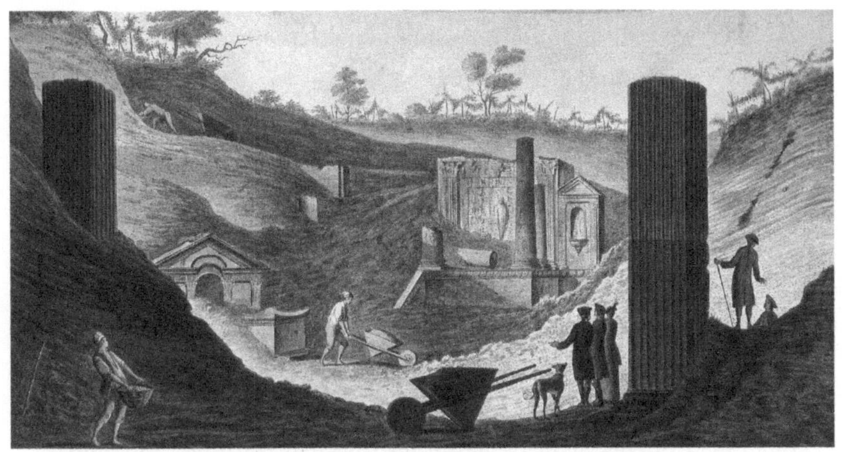

Scientific excavations at Pompeii: discovery of the Temple of Isis, 1776, etching by Pietro Fabris.

rooms in their newly discovered state as a means of public education. A beautiful mosaic, for instance, might satisfy 'the curiosity of the public and of foreigners . . . in seeing some of those mosaic pavements in their proper places and rooms'. Weber also spent an inordinate amount of his time drawing up detailed plans of the ancient underground habitations and public monuments, drawing censure from his colleagues. Camillo Paderni bemoaned Weber's determination to 'draw a plan of Pompeii' and disagreed 'with his Swiss logic that these plans are more necessary and have greater merit than the antiquities which might be found'.[6] Though Weber's ideas were decades ahead of their time, they helped reinforce the Enlightenment impulse to place new knowledge about the world and its history into the hands of collective scholarly bodies that cherished new ideals concerning preservation, science and education. Despite the fact that Weber's work at Herculaneum and Pompeii was heavily criticized at the time, it nonetheless offered an outdoor preview of the sort of approach to art and antiquities that would eventually inform the first two indoor public museums in modern history: the British Museum (1753) and the Louvre (1793).

From the work of Karl Weber at Herculaneum and Pompeii we can see the new scientific standards against which all future scholars would be judged during the course of their excavations and expeditions. First, unlike a diplomat, soldier or dealer, the scholar was supposed to pay close attention to the original context of the excavation site, with the goal of publishing a formal report filled with maps and technical descriptions. Second, any portable antiquities that surfaced during the course of an excavation were not only to be drawn or photographed, but placed in a scientific institution of learning – museum, library or university – that would preserve them for posterity in accordance with the latest conservation methods. This is an important point. To sell such things on the open market to private individuals or to allow wealthy patrons to display them in their mansion was to instantly transform the scholar into a profit-seeking dealer or soldier.

Therefore, if the land in which such antiquities were excavated did not have a public museum designed for preservation and research, scholars considered it entirely appropriate to transport these antiquities to a land where such museums did in fact exist. Crucially, it was not just educated Westerners who subscribed to these new ideals. Some native elites in countries outside Europe also admired this new scholarly ideal, and also thought that their museum-less countries were unfit to keep the material remains of the past. In 1844 Yusuf Hekekyan, a Western-educated Armenian who served as Muhammad Ali's director of the Egyptian School of Engineering, expressed his disappointment at the pasha's failure to live up to the new European ideals. 'Would to God every temple could be transported to England and France by some fairy enchanter', he wrote, 'and some stringent measures taken to preserve them in Egypt.'[7]

To native elites, the scientific credibility of scholars depended on their academic credentials and affiliations with museums or universities. These same elites then duly issued the necessary paperwork authorizing excavations at selected sites, along with the right to call upon assistance from local officials in carrying out their excavations. The next task was to procure a workforce. The digging season in Egypt began in mid-autumn and ended during the spring. This made it relatively easy to recruit willing labourers, since excavation work rarely interfered with the summer harvest. In this sense, any money made while digging for antiquities constituted a form of supplementary income for poor peasant families. Once again, we see the phenomenon of wealth redistribution on display. Flinders Petrie, one of the most famous British Egyptologists during the late nineteenth and early twentieth centuries, once warned his readers that 'everyone will be on the lookout – the sheikh of the village to the smallest child – to find out what can be got out of you.'[8] The foreign archaeologist may not have been a wealthy man himself, but he had the power to redistribute the wealth of his patrons to the poorest members of foreign countries in exchange for an honest day's labour.

On any given day, Petrie estimated that he had somewhere in the vicinity of 100 to 150 workers on his payroll. Their wages, which averaged about twice as much as they would have made in their usual occupations, were paid out once per week. Petrie and other archaeologists in Muslim lands sometimes encountered disputes with local sheikhs, but these disputes were not the result of moral objections over the removal of cultural treasures. Once, the village sheikhs 'tried to stop the people from working, because they did not get the money through their hands'. But the Egyptian *fellahin,* Petrie observed, 'are

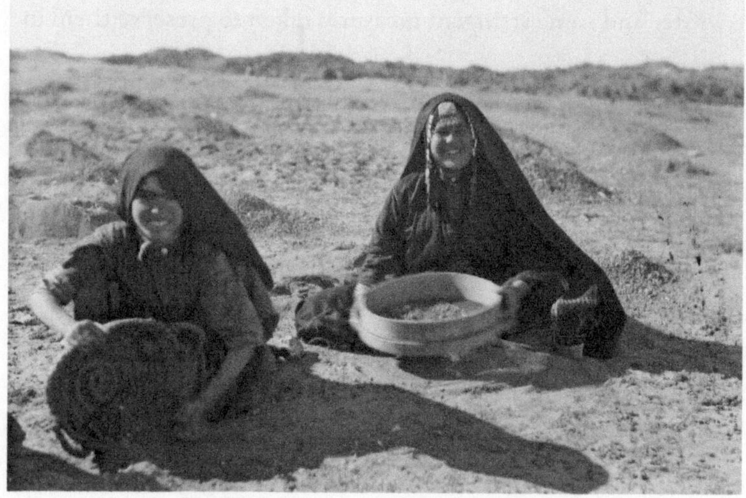

Subsistence diggers in Egypt, *c.* 1920–33.

so glad to get regular pay without any deduction that they say they intend to work, shekhs or no shekhs, as long as there is pay to be had'. According to Petrie, so long as they are 'paid regularly', the *fellahin* 'defy anything short of open violence to stop them'. Worker shortages were rare. In fact, Petrie enjoyed such an abundance of volunteers that he had the luxury of 'discharging for laziness freely', as 'there are so many applicants for work'. Just how many were there? In his detailed study of Petrie's workforce, Stephen Quirke devotes a whopping 72 pages to nothing more than name lists of those Egyptians who appear on Petrie's payrolls. His conclusion is that 'the number grows . . . to such an extent that it might appear, at first sight, to include the whole working population.'[9]

More than 3,200 kilometres (2,000 mi.) away, the German archaeologist Albert von Le Coq oversaw a series of excavations in the Central Asian oasis of Turfan during the first two decades of the twentieth century. When he wasn't hacking away at ancient

Buddhist murals in dark caves, Le Coq spent a great deal of time interacting with the local Muslims upon whom he depended for his workforce, lodging and supplies. Eric Schluessel, a historian at the George Washington University, has recently discovered a fascinating poem written in Uyghur by Mullah Obulmahdi, Le Coq's tutor and guide during his time in Turfan. Schluessel's translation of the poem into English provides a rare unmediated glimpse into the voices of non-Western participants in a Western excavation. Not surprisingly, Obulmahdi spends no time criticizing the unscholarly butchery of pre-Islamic murals that Le Coq oversaw. Instead, he extolled Le Coq as

> a kind and friendly man
> Who has the keys to the treasure in his hand
> If he likes the paper [that is, manuscript] you give him,
>   he will give you money for it
> If he doesn't like the paper, he will give it back.

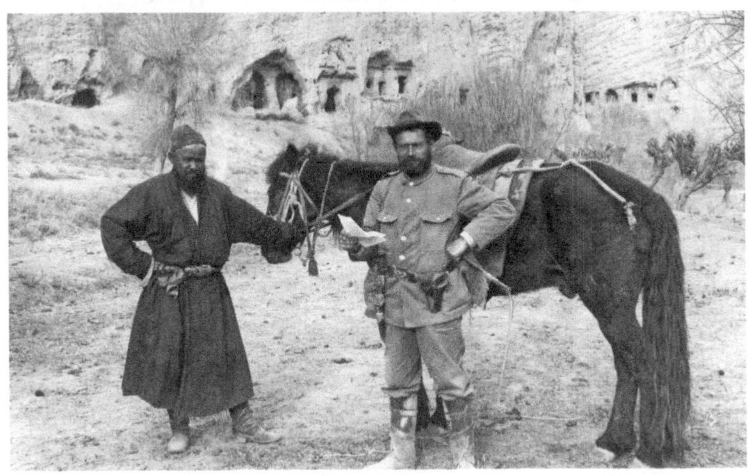

German archaeologist Albert von Le Coq and Uyghur guide, before 1914.

Here again we see the perception among local natives of the Western collector as a type of economic magician, one who turns previously worthless objects into precious cash. Fresco paintings were another object that could become mysteriously lucrative overnight:

> He said, 'I'll pay any good man.'
> We folks looked at the old plaster [and thought],
> For the fresco paintings, no one had ever paid a cent!

The poem ends with an appeal by Obulmahdi for more opportunities to make money during the agricultural slack season:

> You showed me kindness, but then after, what else will
> I do to eat?
> If you would have me in your service, then I would
> come every day;
> And beg in hope from the Efendi [Le Coq] the
> equipment that I need.[10]

Most workers were well paid for their labour, which is why they kept coming back for more. In the many desert sites around the oasis of Turfan, the going rate for unskilled labour appears to be anywhere from one to one and a half silver *mithqals,* a small unit of weight. In his poem, Obulmahdi notes that Le Coq paid a whopping two *mithqals*, while the British archaeologist Aurel Stein occasionally paid up to two and a half *mithqals*. And this was just for unskilled manual labour. The account books of the Yale climatologist Ellsworth Huntington reveal salaries of forty rupees per month for a man named Ibrahim, who served as his chief factotum, translator and guide – an amount more than ten times the going rate for unskilled labour. Other assistants made three to four times above market rate. 'All get good pay,' Huntington wrote to his family back in New Haven, 'and two get what is considered very high, like five or six dollars a day with us.' In addition, once the foreign scholar finished with his excavations and left the area, these newly accessible sites served as a veritable quarry for the locals to return to over and over again in search of additional portable antiquities that they could sell to urban dealers or directly to tourists and scholars. After all, no foreign scholar could remove everything of value from any given site, and he would always depart before the onset of summer heat. In this sense, working for a foreign scholar on an excavation was akin to a paid internship for a future career as a freelance dealer.[11]

But there was more. In addition to attractive wages and the prospect of returning to a partially excavated site at a later date to accumulate one's own private stock for future sale, it was also possible to

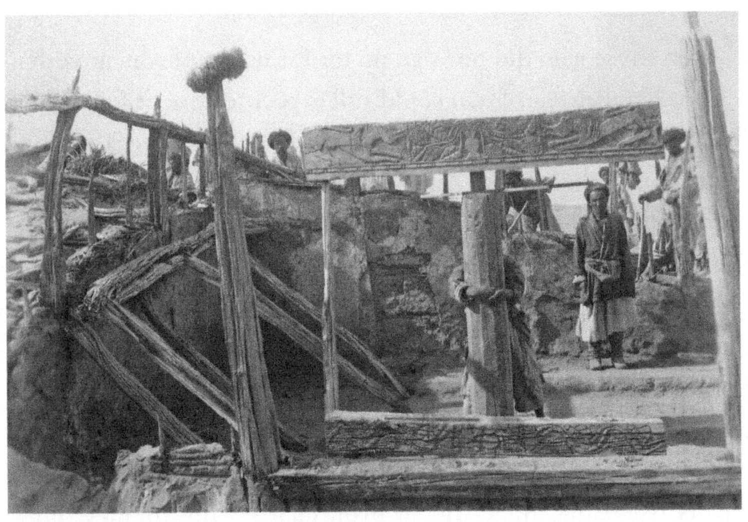

Aurel Stein's desert excavations in Niya, Xinjiang, 1906.

take home extra pay in exchange for uncovering what the scholar regarded as the most valuable artefacts: ancient manuscripts. In 1906 the French sinologist Paul Pelliot told his Uyghur labourers that he would give them an additional reward if they brought him 'paper with characters'. Usually this produced the desired result, but on one humorous occasion his men produced 'a piece of paper with a few lines of writing: it is a fragment of Russian newspaper, they admit then, found on the road'. It was also quite easy to conceal newly unearthed artefacts in the middle of a dig, then sell them on the open market later – or sometimes back to a less-than-vigilant employer. 'Despite all the surveillance', Pelliot once wrote, 'it is difficult to prevent a worker from sliding a small piece, just revealed by his *ketman* [spade], into a fold of his clothes.'[12] Thus an enterprising and clever subsistence digger could generate multiple streams of revenue through his association with an archaeologist's excavation: wages, rewards, artefacts concealed during a dig and artefacts recovered after a dig.

Even those who did not sign up for formal employment with a scholar like Petrie or Stein could still expect to benefit financially from the scholar's mere presence. The archives of some of the more meticulous archaeologists still preserve the account books they used to record all of their daily expenses. This should not surprise us, since they were spending someone else's money and knew they could be held accountable for unexplained expenditures. Stein's account books for his digs in the deserts of northwestern China are particularly complete. To take the ledger lines of a single random month (July 1914) as an example, we see that Stein paid members of the local community for the following goods and services: tent pegs, leather repairs, telegrams, animal fodder, living quarters, fuel for fires, shoeing of ponies (including the cost of nails), cart rentals, cotton for packing, gifts for a monastery, sheep, messengers, oats, food, wooden cases, straw, escorts, ponies and yak rental, and a guide – and most of these expenses appear over and over again, for months or years at a time. Viewed in this light, it is little wonder that the arrival of a Western archaeologist was frequently welcomed with open arms by the local community: nearly everyone, regardless of whether or not they were willing to dig for him in the desert, stood to profit handsomely from his manifold needs and bottomless bank account. To describe the arrival of a Western archaeologist in a remote community as an economic stimulus package is to indulge in only a small degree of hyperbole.

And these were just the tangible economic compensations on tap. There were also intangible ones as well. If a native labourer, guide or translator happened to prove particularly useful or reliable, the Western scholar would often recommend him, formally or informally, to local elites who were in a position to offer him lucrative career prospects previously undreamt of. One of the most dramatic examples of this phenomenon can be found in the letters of Ellsworth Huntington, who in March 1906 decided to lobby on behalf of Da'ud, one of his favourite Uyghur assistants, during an audience with the provincial Chinese governor:

> His supreme ambition is to become a *beg* [village headman], not a big *beg*, but a little one with some simple work adapted to his ability. As he has been very faithful in spite of his shortcomings I asked the Fu-tai [governor] to give him such an office, that is to give him a letter to that effect to the local Amban [official] at Keriya, telling at the same time what sort of man he is, faithful and honest, but not especially clever. The Fu-tai promised to do so and when he called on me asked to see the

> man. Poor Da'ud, most horribly frightened, was brought in, and after falling on his knees at the door and bowing his close-shaven head to the ground half a dozen times advanced nearer to be looked at. I suppose it was the great experience of his life, one that he will boast of till his death, for as Ibrahim said, a man like that could not procure a personal interview with the Futai if he paid 5,000 dollars.[13]

In this revealing passage, we see Ibrahim, another one of Huntington's guides, projecting what is essentially a priceless valuation upon the career networking opportunity that Da'ud had just received. According to Ibrahim, not even U.S.$5,000 – more money than Da'ud would have ever made in several lifetimes – could have bought what Huntington just procured for him. Such informal promotions were common during archaeological excavations and expeditions, with most of them appearing in the form of letters of recommendation rather than an exclusive audience with a Chinese governor.

It should hardly surprise us, then, to find that men whose entire livelihoods were transformed for the better through association with a Western archaeologist would continue to cherish that relationship for the rest of their lives. This was certainly the case with Jiang Xiaowan, one of Stein's educated Chinese assistants who helped him identify Chinese-language manuscripts and to correspond with local Chinese officials during his second expedition to northwestern China in 1906–8. Stein was so enamoured of Jiang's eager and insightful assistance over a gruelling three-year period that he gifted him a silver watch upon conclusion of the expedition. It was engraved with the following words: 'Presented by Dr. M. A. Stein to Chiang Ssu-yieh [Jiang] as a token of sincere regard and in grateful remembrance of his devoted scholarly services during explorations in Chinese

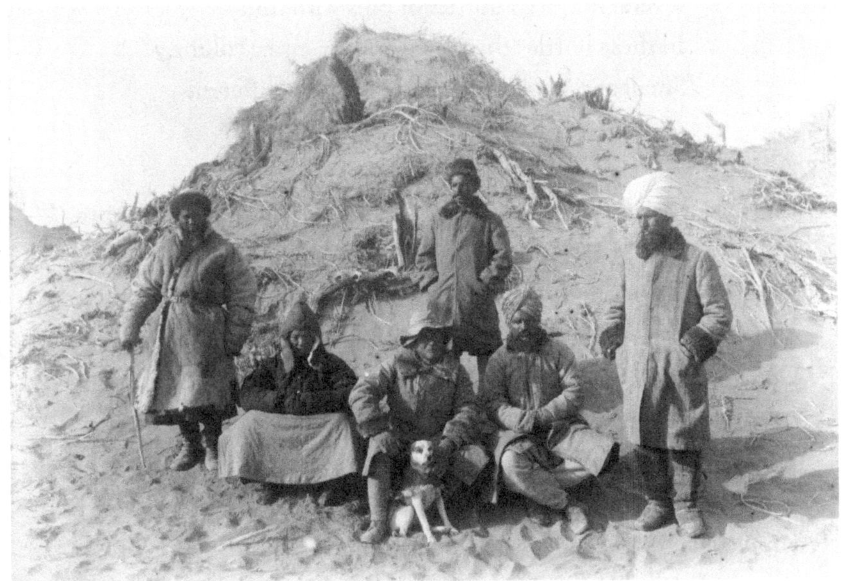

Aurel Stein's expedition team, 1907.

Turkestan, 1906–08.' We know that this watch was important to Jiang because he authored a will in which he warned his son not to sell it, for it was a symbol of one of the greatest memories of his life. After the expedition, Stein secured lifelong employment for Jiang in the British consulate in Kashgar, a post that was taken up by his son after his death. And when Jiang finally passed away in 1922, Stein sent 300 rupees from India to help pay for the cost of transporting his coffin back to his homeland in inner China.[14]

Last but not least, we would be remiss not to mention one of the less obvious forms of intangible compensation that Western archaeologists made freely available to the local populace: medicine. Most Westerners gave out pills, salves and basic medical examinations for free, fully aware that this was a great way to spread goodwill. In his poem about Le Coq, Mullah Obulmahdi wrote about the

> several hundred bottles of pills with him
> In these bottles there were pills of every color
> Small and large they were, each for a different
> ailment.

Of these, perhaps the most titillating category of pills were aphrodisiacs. In 1906 Paul Pelliot wrote in his diary about an elderly Uyghur guide named Qoutloug Beg, whom he described as 'a great womanizer despite his age'. After telling Pelliot all about his dreams of beautiful women, Qoutloug Beg asked Pelliot a veiled question. 'He would like to know today whether he can still expect a summer of Saint-Martin from our pharmacy.' A 'summer of Saint-Martin' is a French euphemism for unseasonably warm weather late in the year, roughly equivalent to an English 'Indian summer'. Pelliot quickly caught the man's drift. 'Despite the precedent for the Duke of Richelieu,' he wrote, referring to a lecherous old French aristocrat from the eighteenth century, 'I do not dare to promise this to him.' Stein received similar requests from elderly Chinese officials who told him that they still hoped to father a son in spite of their advanced years.[15] It is thus entirely possible that some museum artefacts, far from being the result of imperialist plunder, ended up inside glass cabinets because they were exchanged for an early twentieth-century version of Viagra.

Not everyone was enamoured of the Western archaeologist, however. Though widespread voluntary consent was an indispensable ingredient for any successful archaeological venture, there was still plenty of room for disenchantment. But the source of this disenchantment might surprise us, for it had nothing to do with debates over cultural sovereignty or laments for lost artefacts. Rather, it was almost entirely rooted in what we might today characterize as workplace disputes. That is, whenever the real or perceived hazards and discomforts of the expedition trail began to outweigh the suite of compensations offered by the Western archaeologist in the minds of the locals, they would register their discontent by voting with their feet and shunning his digs. In his unpublished field diaries, Aurel Stein recorded repeated instances of complaints or refusals to work over such perceived dangers as 'wild Tibetans', dragons, jinns, overly long marches, bad food, early morning wake-up calls, cold weather, uncomfortable tents, temperamental camels and snoring tentmates. In April 1907 Ram Singh, an Indian surveyor contracted by Stein to map the route of his expedition throughout northwestern China, ticked off several of these irritations in a laundry list of complaints that he submitted to Stein: 'too long marches . . . cooking shared with Naik – & latter's snoring; bad quarters . . . no superior pony, and – too little ease & comfort'.[16]

On other occasions, a lack of enthusiasm among the local populace for tapping into the archaeologist's purse could be explained by reasons entirely unrelated even to the physical aggravations of employment. According to Paul Pelliot, two recurring events tended to undermine all efforts at recruitment: market days and religious holidays. 'I had also wanted workers today, Monday,' he wrote in his diary in May 1907, 'but this is the main day of the bazaar; there are scarcely five or six; I have postponed the resumption of the excavations until tomorrow.' Here we see the considerable resources and will of the Western scholar completely thwarted by something as simple as market day – and there was nothing Pelliot could do about it. But Muslim holidays were even worse. 'This evening ends the month of Ramadan,' he noted in November 1906. 'There is, therefore, no counting on any workman for two days; the whole village will be in the mosque or in visits and feasts.' And then there was the occasional wife or mother who refused to let her husband or son risk his health in a dusty dig. One man, 'yielding to his wife's tears, renounced his departure', while another told Stein that he could no longer accompany him due to the 'request of his old mother'.[17]

So there *were* some people who offered principled resistance to the agenda of Western archaeologists. It just wasn't the sort of principles or resistance that retroactive nationalist discourses have conditioned us to expect. When Western scholars were turned away, it was not because locals thought they were stealing their country's cultural heritage – it was because they didn't want to do battle with a desert jinn, listen to their snoring tentmate, miss out on the gossip of the marketplace, sit on a lumpy camel or deal with a relative's tears. These were some of the many ways in which the less privileged lower classes could – and did – say no. And whenever this happened, foreign scholars were forced to respect that answer and either abandon or revise their plans in order to address the grievances that their would-be labourers actually cared about.

Nearly all of the ins and outs of an archaeological dig summarized thus far would have applied equally to both a stationary excavation like Petrie's and to a mobile expedition like Stein's. This makes sense, since an expedition was really just a series of excavations undertaken over the course of a geographically contiguous journey. And yet the fact that mobile expeditions were so much more logistically complicated than a stationary excavation – which was already complex enough – meant that there were some unique features of an expedition that bear further scrutiny. First, they were far more dangerous and physically taxing than an excavation. Whereas an excavator usually chose the most favourable seasons for digging and then retreated to more moderate climes for the intense summer months, those who undertook an expedition could be gone for years at a time, with little to no break from their constant labours and residence in a culturally alien land. Sooner or later, serious injuries were almost guaranteed to sideline members of expeditions in remote areas far from adequate medical care. During his four expeditions to northwestern China, Stein lost a toe to frostbite in the Himalayas and narrowly escaped death when his horse reared back and crashed to the ground, pinning his leg underneath.

All of this hardship, however, did make for a good story. This is why the annals of archaeology are dominated by popular accounts of Western expeditions, despite the fact that these make up only a tiny percentage of the collecting activities of Western scholars. In the public eye, gripping narratives of adventurous expeditions have come to dominate our impressions of archaeologists. To name just a few, the American palaeontologist Roy Chapman Andrews, Swedish geographer Sven Hedin and American historian Hiram Bingham have been portrayed as larger-than-life figures in their own best-selling books and those of their breathless admirers. Their masculine yarns of scientific risk-taking led in turn to opportunities for commercial endorsements. Hedin once lent his name and likeness to an advertisement for a bottle of French beef extract, an illustration of which was superimposed next to a colourful caravan of camels in Tibet. Andrews, for his part, promoted everything from Savage rifles to Dodge motorcars. One typical full-page spread appeared in the May 1938 edition of *Better Homes and Gardens*:

> In the Gobi Desert, Dodge always came through under circumstances where a single failure would have meant slow death from starvation and thirst. No wonder that not only myself but Mrs. Andrews as well, appreciate the even greater dependability that has been built into our new 1938 Dodge!

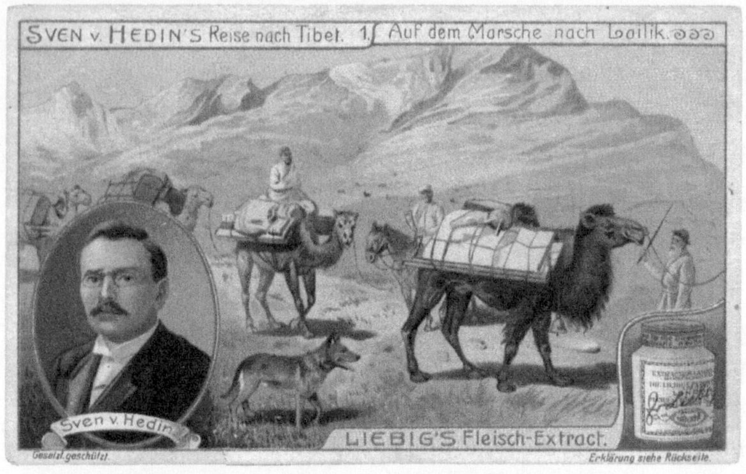

Sven Hedin trading card advertising beef extract, *c.* 1908.

Still, their credibility as scholars derived not from these lucrative commercial indulgences, but rather from their scientific publications – and each of these men took time to publish dense, multi-volume tomes filled with technical reports alongside their rousing accounts of masculine machismo. For our purposes here, the takeaway point is that scholars who undertook rigorous archaeological expeditions tended to achieve a modest amount of fame in their own lifetimes, with their names recognized far beyond narrow circles of academia and museums. They were respected, admired and celebrated not only for their adventurous exploits on the ground, but for their scholarly analysis in their learned books. Men like Hedin and Stein were scientific celebrities on camel-back, doing things that no one had ever done before – or had even thought possible. In this sense, they were the astronauts of their day.

Of course, it may not come as a great surprise to learn that Western journalists, advertisers, scholars, museums and publishers were eager to embrace these bombastic archaeologists in their home countries.

After all, isn't this just a simple case of arrogant and racist Westerners promoting the colonialist activities of a thinly veiled Western cultural imperialist drawn from their own chauvinist ranks? Perhaps. But what if we had access to the voices not merely of illiterate non-Western peasants eager to make money, but educated, wealthy non-Western elites? Some critics will find it easy to dismiss the enthusiastic cooperation of impoverished Muslim and Chinese peasants, since poverty can make a person do almost anything simply to survive another day. But this charge cannot be levelled quite so easily at those powerful native elites whose financial portfolios often exceeded that of the Western scholar with whom they interacted. In most parts of the world, the unmediated thoughts of native elites regarding the activities of Western archaeologists are difficult to find, if they exist at all. Either these elites were content to communicate in speech alone and did not record their thoughts in writing at all or they were already educated in the West and preferred to document their careers in a European language by the time they appear on the historian's radar. Another possibility is that historians simply haven't been looking hard enough: it seems difficult to believe that Arabic, Persian or Thai documentation was never produced by native elites throughout the Muslim and Southeast Asian worlds for Western expeditions during the nineteenth century.

There is one major exception, however, and it is to be found in China. By the time the first Western archaeologists began to undertake expeditions in northwestern China in the 1890s, the ranks of the reigning Qing bureaucracy were still filled with classically educated Confucian officials who had only a superficial familiarity with Western learning. These were not rustic illiterates, desperate to get rich quick by selling out their country. They were among the most highly educated, financially prosperous men in all of Asia, and were committed to protecting their country from Western imperialists. Not only that, but unlike elites nearly everywhere else in the world, these Chinese officials also cherished the same stuff that Western archaeologists were removing from their country. It stands to reason, then, that such men would have had a different response to the scholarly agents of Western imperialism. After all, they had no need to tap the archaeologist's purse (and would probably be arrested on charges of corruption by their own government if they had). This means they were thus entirely immune to the chief form of compensation – economic – that regularly motivated their poorer subjects to dig in the sand on behalf of foreigners.

Unfortunately, those hoping to find an echo of present-day critiques of imperialist theft in the original Chinese-language documentation regarding Western archaeologists are likely to be sorely disappointed. For if anything, the Confucian elites of China were even more enamoured of the Western scholar who braved their remote desert jurisdictions in search of a bodhisattva's head than were the impoverished lower classes. Our first piece of evidence on this score is dated to April 1901, when Aurel Stein began to wrap up the first of his four expeditions to the northwestern Chinese province known as Xinjiang. Han Yaoguang, the Chinese prefect in the oasis of Keriya, was required to submit a report up the chain of command to his superiors in the Qing bureaucracy providing a description of Stein's activities. In addition to a host of mundane minutiae relating to Stein's lodgings, food, social interactions and other movements, Han also chose to include his personal opinion of Stein. 'He is an outstanding person', Han wrote, 'of much culture and refinement' (*wei ren wenwen jinya, yi shi jiezhe*).[18]

Han was not alone in these sentiments; he was merely the most concise. The very next year, Rao Yingqi, the Chinese governor of

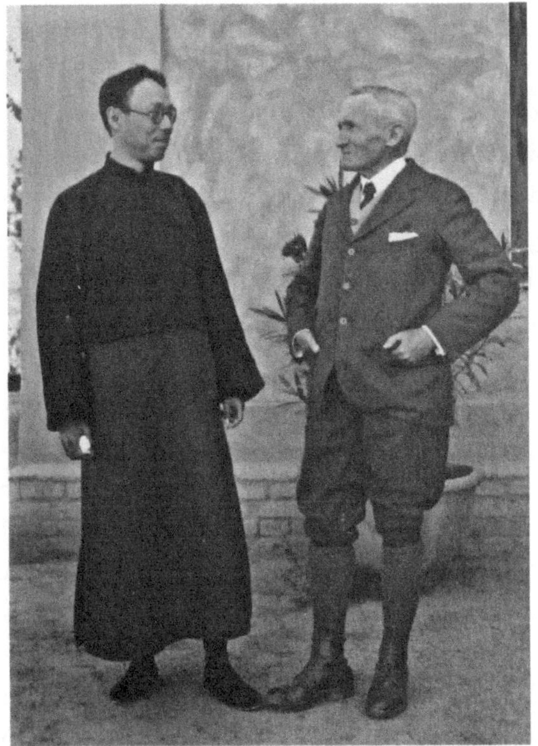
Aurel Stein with Chinese official Pan Zuhuan (son of provincial official Pan Zhen), 1930.

Xinjiang, heard about the English-language publication of Stein's preliminary report for his first expedition and commissioned a Chinese translation from one of his aides. This should not surprise us, since educated Confucians were just as interested in the long history of their own civilization as educated Westerners were. And yet in this document, which was first identified and translated into English by Imre Galambos, a professor of Chinese at the University of Cambridge, we find not a hint of jealously or enmity anywhere within its pages. In comments appended to the end of the Chinese translation, Wan Rong, the translator, describes the governor as having 'highly praised' Stein's report, claiming that 'scholars fond of antiquities competed with each other for copying it, eager to enjoy the privilege of reading it first.' As for Stein himself, Wan characterized him as a 'highly refined gentleman' (*boya junzi*) who spent just under two years 'incessantly climbing mountains, traversing rivers, and seeking out antiquities and ancient sites. He tracked every matter to its source and investigated its nature.' He then ridiculed some of his 'ignorant' colleagues in the provincial government who chose to 'take no notice' of Stein's accomplishments:

> The natural sciences of the West are all developed on the basis of observation; their weapons and technology are advanced through learning. Aspirations of studying natural phenomena lead to wealth and power, but the principle of going from studying to political might seems coincidental to people. They all marvel at the natural sciences and are in awe of Western weapons and technology, yet when it comes to seeing Mr Stein crossing mountains and rivers, or travelling through the desert, they laugh at his folly. This is just being ignorant![19]

Here we see Wan criticizing the long-standing bias among educated Confucian gentlemen against physical exertion and labour, for that was what illiterate, filthy peasants did. But the larger point is that Wan was using Stein as a rhetorical example of what a modern man of science is supposed to be doing with his time and energy. These Chinese officials wanted to discover the secrets of Western wealth and power so that they could resist Western imperialism – and lo and behold, here was a vigorous paragon of the latest Western scientific methods giving them a personal demonstration of how the West amassed its wealth and power right before their eyes. Of course, the specific example on display was the discipline of archaeology, but this was interpreted merely as one representative branch of Western science in its entirety.

The fact that Stein's archaeological demonstration included the removal of art and antiquities from the desert sands of Xinjiang was immaterial to these Chinese officials, since all of Wan's readers grew up in a world where the earth did not love its treasures and finders keepers ruled the day. What mattered is that Stein had shown this group of Chinese officials in Xinjiang the path to making China stronger through the lessons he had demonstrated via the Western branch of science known as archaeology. And Wan wanted to make sure his colleagues in the provincial bureaucracy were paying attention. Seen from this perspective, it seems strange that Stein is so often regarded as an agent of Western cultural imperialism today, both within China and without. On the contrary, just one century ago the most highly educated and prosperous Chinese in the entire country saw in Stein's expedition not a sinister imposition of foreign imperialism, but rather an altruistic and admirable display of the scientific keys to catching up with the leading Western powers of the day. The Chinese translation of Stein's report, along with Wan's editorial in its postface, might be compared to the activist approach of a CEO of our own day and age, one who forwards a glowing profile about the business practices and ethos of some rival entrepreneur to every employee in the company, appended with the observation that 'this is what we should be doing here.'

If this was all the Chinese-language documentation we possessed about Western archaeologists, it would be thin but thought-provoking. But there is so much more. From 1907 to 1915, during the height of Western expeditions to Xinjiang, Stein and Pelliot received dozens of letters from Chinese officials whom they met in

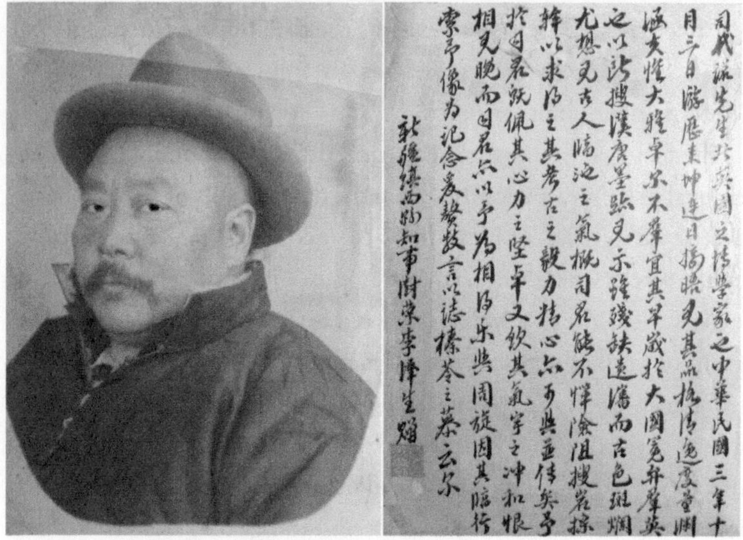

Letter and photograph given to Stein by Chinese official Li Shurong, 1914.

between their excavations. Did they know what Stein and Pelliot were removing from their country? Absolutely. In 1914 Li Shurong, the district magistrate of Barikol, thanked Stein for allowing him 'to see the ink traces of the Han and Tang dynasties that you have collected'. Longtime provincial official Pan Zhen also expressed his gratitude to Stein for giving him the opportunity to 'cast my gaze back over several thousand years, as if the ancients were standing right before me'. Stein, who knew far more intuitively than we do today that none of these Chinese officials would feel entitled to lay claim to any of the objects he had uncovered within their jurisdictions, freely gave away copies of his books about previous expeditions. The reason these gifts are worth noting is because Stein's books were filled with photographs of what he had already removed on prior expeditions in years past. Did men like Pan Zhen regard these photographs as belated evidence of a crime, as many critics of

Western museums today do? 'I have received the book you sent as a gracious gift,' wrote Pan, then serving as circuit intendant for the Aksu region, in 1908, 'and have already browsed through it. Truly, it is a work that is destined to be cherished and passed around, and it elicits a special admiration.' In another letter, Pan described them as 'expansive books of great importance that encompass everything you have experienced, be it the traces of the ancients or the customs of our contemporaries'. In 1913 Keriya magistrate Dai Chengmo declared that his 'deep admiration' for Stein was based on 'the collection of books he has authored and annotated'. In 1925 Shule magistrate Wang Min informed Stein that 'all the books you have written about your expeditions in Xinjiang are destined to become the subject of deep respect among learned men, who will compete with one another to purchase and read them.'[20]

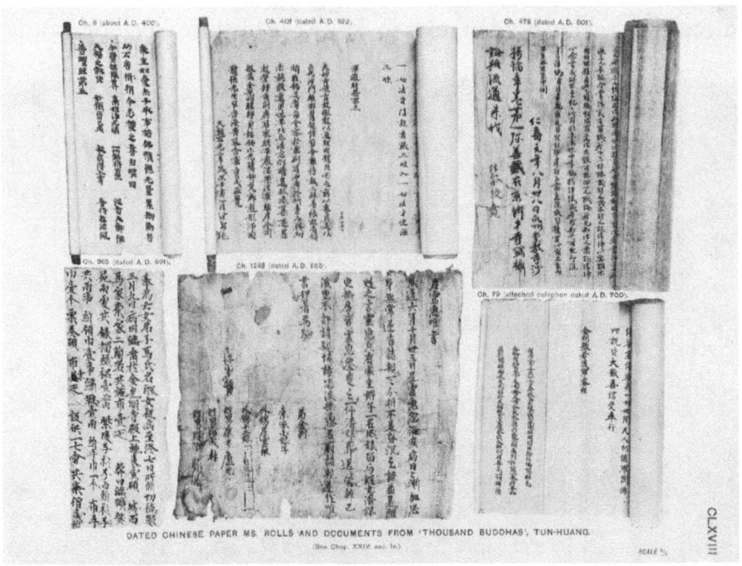

Facsimiles of Chinese documents removed by Stein from China, included in his published book *Serindia* (1921).

Not only did these officials know what Stein and Pelliot were taking abroad, but they looked forward to hearing about the new scholarly discoveries that would result from transporting these antiquities to a site better suited to their preservation and study. In 1908 the Manchu prince Zailan, then serving out a term of exile in the provincial capital of Ürümchi, wrote Pelliot a mushy letter in which he recalled how they had 'rejoiced in wine and food' and 'held hands as we engaged in pleasant conversation about antiquity and our present age'. Unfortunately for Zailan, Pelliot's subsequent departure meant that he had 'not stopped mourning [his] absence'. And yet news that Pelliot had continued onward to the Mogao Grottoes at Dunhuang, where he could 'tour the ancient grottoes with joy, gaze upon the Buddhist relics with reverence, and trace the remnants of steles with your hand', brought Zailan much satisfaction. The exiled prince hoped that Pelliot, 'an erudite scholar and lover of antiquity', would succeed in 'taking hold of texts to verify the histories'. Pelliot's study

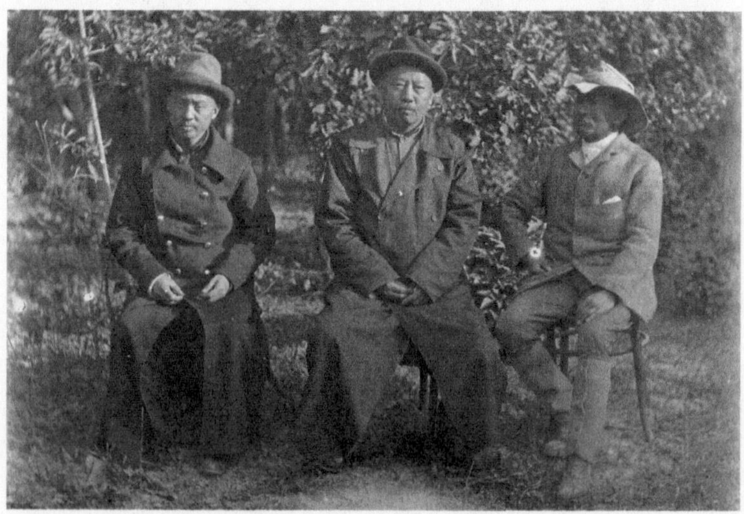

Aurel Stein with Chinese official Zhu Ruichi (middle), 1915.

of 'these forgotten manuscripts will contribute to the progress of humanity and shine a glorious light on our frontier landscape'.[21]

Such paeans have merely scratched the surface of Chinese admiration for the Western archaeologists in their midst. 'Be it the traces of the ancients or the customs of our contemporaries,' Pan Zhen added in another letter, 'there is not one that you have failed thoroughly to uncover and investigate, presenting them in expansive books of great importance that encompass everything you have experienced. This is truly worthy of an admiration that knows no bounds.' Shule magistrate Wang Min believed that Stein's expeditions and books had greatly enriched his knowledge of Chinese history, and for that he was grateful. 'The history of Xinjiang in China since Han and Tang times has also benefitted from your investigations,' wrote Wang. 'These are significant accomplishments.' He was certain that Stein's best-selling books would lead to so many reprints in order to satisfy reader demand that the resulting stress on paper supplies would be 'not unlike when paper became expensive in Luoyang' – a time-worn allusion to popular literary creations in Chinese history whose feverish recopying in the imperial capital exhausted the city's entire supply of paper.[22]

Nor did any of these officials believe that Stein should be locked up and thrown in prison upon his return to England. In 1908 Zhu Ruichi, the prefect of Guma, told Stein that he could 'imagine that you are returning to your home country in a carriage pulled by piebald horses to have an audience with your king, who will grant you untold awards and infinite honours'. Zhu, of course, wanted to be first in line to shake Stein's hand. 'I would like to congratulate you in advance on your imminent promotion.' When Zhu later heard that Stein had 'encountered snowcapped mountain peaks and a bitter cold air that pierced through to the bone and rendered all clothing immaterial' on his passage through the Himalayas – where Stein lost a toe to frostbite – he did not indulge in a smug dose of anti-imperialist *Schadenfreude*. Instead, he confessed to feelings of the deepest 'grief' and 'sorrow'. Upon further reflection, however, Zhu's thoughts turned to – what else? – admiration.

> What I mourn is the thought of the hardships you must endure while scaling mountains and fording bodies of water, and of the difficult straits in which you continually place yourself. What I admire, however, is your stern fortitude and valiant resolve.

In the final analysis, Zhu was immeasurably grateful merely to be able to say that he had met and hosted such an impressive scholar. 'Everywhere you set your foot, dear Sir,' Zhu wrote, 'becomes famous, from the lustre you confer on the sands of the Gobi to the distinction you confer on the peaks of the Kunlun.'[23]

In 1914 Barikol magistrate Li Shurong expressed similar sentiments after calling on Stein in person seven times over the course of the six days he spent in town. 'Across multiple meetings over several days,' Li later wrote in his letter to Stein,

> I was able to see that you are a man of outstanding character and broad mind, unsurpassed in elegance and refinement . . . You, Mr Stein, do not shirk from any danger or obstacle in scouring grottoes or collecting wooden slips. In pursuit of these things, you practise archaeology with a stunning perseverance and thoroughness that is unheard of.[24]

As we can see from this passage, Li knew Stein was removing ancient 'wooden slips' inscribed with Chinese characters – and he wished him godspeed. In 1913 the Keriya magistrate Dai Chengmo placed Stein in the upper echelon of the greatest men he had ever met across the entire globe:

> In years gone by, I travelled through such countries as Russia, Germany and Austria, as well as to the Caspian, Black and Mediterranean Seas, through whose various ports I passed. I made the acquaintance of a great many exceptional people, yet the English Minister for Education Aurel Stein, whom I did not befriend until the *guichou* year [1913] when in the role of magistrate of Keriya, would be the most excellent of them all: proper of character, refined of learning, versed in the ancient and familiar with the modern. My admiration for him, having viewed the collection of books he has authored and annotated, is deep indeed.[25]

Well, this is awkward. After all, Stein has become something of a nationalist piñata among Chinese critics of Western imperialism today. As recently as 2022, Wang Jiqing, a historian at Lanzhou University, wrote that any suggestion that the objects Stein and other Western archaeologists removed from China could be the result of anything other than rapacious imperialist plunder constituted nothing more than 'shameless excuses'.[26] And yet in support of his counter-argument, Wang cannot cite a single instance of any Chinese person expressing even the slightest critique of Stein or any other Western archaeologist in their own day and age. There is a simple reason for this: such evidence does not exist. In my own study of early twentieth-century Chinese discourse on Western archaeologists, I failed to uncover a single instance of criminalizing language to describe what Stein and other archaeologists were doing in China.

Instead, the removal of art and antiquities abroad was consistently mediated in Chinese through unambiguously neutral verbs: 'obtain' (*de*), 'collect' (*huo*), 'take' (*qu*), 'transport' (*yun*), 'send' (*ji*), 'carry' (*xie, dai*), 'excavate' (*jue*) and 'dig' (*wa*).[27] And why shouldn't the Chinese use such neutral terms? After all, they did not yet regard any of these activities as theft. Even as late as 1923 the noted geologist Ding Wenjiang told Roy Chapman Andrews that his Asiatic Expedition to Chinese-controlled Inner Mongolia 'has every right to leave its collections – even the geological and palaeontological collections – in any museum or institution it may consider best suitable'.[28]

So it turns out that some of the most widely touted 'Western imperialist thieves' in modern Chinese history were actually regarded as esteemed scientific celebrities in their own day and age – and not just in the West, but in China as well. As a result, there is a great deal of irony in the ubiquitous calls for cultural restitution that define our present age. Such strident calls for the repatriation of objects in Western museums are often premised on the conviction that the return of artefacts will restore the lost voices of a nation's ancestors. And yet in the one substantial case study available to us in which authentic, unmediated 'lost voices' have been thoroughly recovered – the Chinese case – we find that they stand in stark opposition to the shrill accusations of their nationalist descendants. In other words, proponents of repatriation, in claiming to speak on behalf of oppressed, marginalized victims of Western imperialism whose voices they themselves have made no attempt to recover, have in fact done more to silence, efface and dismiss the very same voices of those ancestors than any Western archaeologist ever did.

To return to the analogy first invoked in the Introduction, when we treat history as a living will, we must be prepared to accept that the hopes, dreams and concerns of our forefathers may not align with the hopes, dreams and concerns of their descendants. Poor Muslim and Chinese labourers, along with wealthy Chinese elites, all eagerly gravitated towards Western archaeological expeditions in hopes of fulfilling some personal or collective goal – economic, political, social, cultural – onto which they placed a far higher valuation at the time than they did onto the objects being removed from their country. This rational calculus, which was reached voluntarily and without the threat of coercion, made perfect sense at the time – and to any historian who cares to look. To stand here today and claim that a poor Uyghur guide like Da'ud should have valued a tattered Buddhist manuscript over the once-in-a-lifetime opportunity to pull himself out of abject poverty is to impose the righteous privilege of a well-fed armchair historian onto long-dead historical figures. The same goes for those wealthy and powerful Chinese officials who were so endeared of Stein and Pelliot. Who are we to tell them that they were wrong to believe more in the promise of Western science than in the supposed inviolability of a Chinese nation whose very existence few of them would have even acknowledged? It is one thing to play the part of a historical ventriloquist when the voices of the dead are unrecoverable or simply unknown. It is a moral transgression of quite another order, however, to put the ideological agendas of a later generation into the mouths of the deceased when their voices are both recoverable and known.

So how did we get from a world in which almost no one viewed Western archaeologists as imperialist thieves to a world in which nearly everyone regards them as such? The answer is simple: Western scholars became thieves once non-Westerners became Westernized and turned the Western discourse of 'priceless' art and antiquities back on its originators. As we have seen, no one other than a Western scholar collecting objects for deposit in a museum, library or university regarded these objects as 'priceless'. Even if someone other than a Western scholar said something was priceless, this was merely hyperbole, since their subsequent actions nearly always betrayed their words: antiquities were sold, traded, cut up, smashed, hoarded, gifted and bequeathed with mundane regularity. In other words, they all had a price, even if that price was not always articulated in bald monetary terms. It was only Western scholars affiliated with an Enlightenment institution of learning who said that the objects they collected were priceless emblems of various groups of humanity and should be placed into a museum for preservation and study in perpetuity, without the possibility of further sale.

This is why Western scholars were so persistent in the collection of non-Western artefacts, and why everyone with whom they came into contact in the source country was so willing to oblige them for the right price. For only those who viewed art and antiquities as priceless would be willing to spend enormous sums of money on an excavation, expedition or other form of acquisition for which they expected to receive no additional financial remuneration beyond their fixed salary. And only when they encountered people who did not share their priceless view of old things long buried in the ground or disintegrating on the surface of the earth, the sole possible point of conflict concerned the amount of compensation that Western scholars would need to dole out in order to exceed local valuations of the objects targeted for removal. Once these negotiations were completed, logistical support for their operations would materialize. The amount and form of compensation necessary to satisfy local demands was unique to each time, place and person: cash for Egyptian *fellahin*, an audience with the Chinese governor for a Uyghur guide, or a promise to shed new light on Han and Tang history for those wealthy officials infatuated with Stein.

But this rate of exchange only worked so long as the two parties in question held different valuations of the objects slated for removal. So the question now becomes: when did the non-Western party start to regard art and antiquities as priceless in the same way that Western scholars did – that is, as absolutely unsuitable for further sale or private transfer? For once that happens and both sides regard the same object as priceless, negotiations over a mutually palatable form of compensation are doomed to fail – for nothing can ever truly exceed a genuine 'priceless' valuation. We have already observed that the public institutions that embodied the Enlightenment ideals of science, preservation and education were almost entirely responsible for projecting the Western valuation of priceless onto objects that entered their collections. Of course, there was an ugly imperialist ideology behind this process: when the alabaster sarcophagus of the ancient Egyptian pharaoh Seti I came into the possession of the Soane Museum in London, it absolutely served to reinforce British claims to be the most enlightened stewards of Egypt's past – and possibly, depending on how things played out, its future.

But now the final piece of the puzzle comes into focus. Namely, when did the Enlightenment institution of the public museum and its rhetoric of priceless artefacts begin to appear in non-Western lands, that is, the same non-Western lands where Western scholars were fond of collecting previously negotiable objects that the locals did not regard as priceless? Once this last question is answered, the genealogy of a discourse of criminalization towards Western archaeologists can finally be written.

Fortunately, we already have the answers. In the early nineteenth century, the Egyptian pasha Muhammad Ali gave voice to the first echo of Western Enlightenment ideals regarding the disposition of ancient ruins. On 15 August 1835 Muhammad Ali issued a decree that lamented the 'destruction of ancient edifices' throughout Egypt and forbade the export abroad of antiquities. He also outlined a vision for a European-style museum in Cairo. 'It is also well known that the Europeans have buildings for keeping antiquities,' he wrote, along with 'stones covered with paintings and inscriptions, and other similar objects... carefully conserved there and shown to the inhabitants of the country as well as to travelers ... such establishments bring great renown to the countries which have them.'[29] Of course, the pasha did almost nothing to inject substance into this decree, continuing to quarry ancient ruins for his own construction projects and gifting away an obelisk to France. Nevertheless, a Western seed had been planted, and as new ideas about museums, preservation and education began to take root, the perceived value of antiquities among non-Western politicians and intellectuals would continue to rise until it finally matched the Western valuation of priceless.

In 1846, just a decade after Muhammad Ali's pronouncement, the Imperial Ottoman Museum opened its doors in Istanbul. Converted from an old Greek Orthodox church, this was the first museum to be founded outside Europe and America. Though it originally held an eclectic display of ancient Ottoman swords and wax mannequins of the recently abolished military caste known as the Janissaries, within a few decades it would be moved into a brand-new Graeco-Roman style building and filled with Greek, Roman and Byzantine antiquities. This tendency to display the same sort of antiquities that Western museums valued was a direct result of the Western education that those involved in the creation and administration of these non-Western museums had received. The Ottoman intellectual and archaeologist Osman Hamdi Bey (1842–1910) is a case in point. After studying law and art in Paris, Osman returned to Istanbul and was eventually appointed as director of the Imperial

Ottoman Museum. Over the course of his lengthy career, Osman regularly criticized conservative Muslim values, painted 'Orientalist' depictions of Islamic subjects and built up a museum collection that privileged the antiquities of pre-Islamic Mediterranean civilizations to the near exclusion of Islamic artefacts.[30]

Already we can see the intellectual contours of the Egyptian and Turkish mimicry of Western ideologies regarding art and antiquities taking shape. The basis of non-Western interest in the same sort of antiquities that the Westerners themselves valued was not predicated on the popularization of the sort of past that the Muslim masses cherished. If that had been the case, the Imperial Ottoman Museum would not have been built within a bone-white Graeco-Roman colonnade and stuffed with pre-Islamic artefacts. Instead, it would

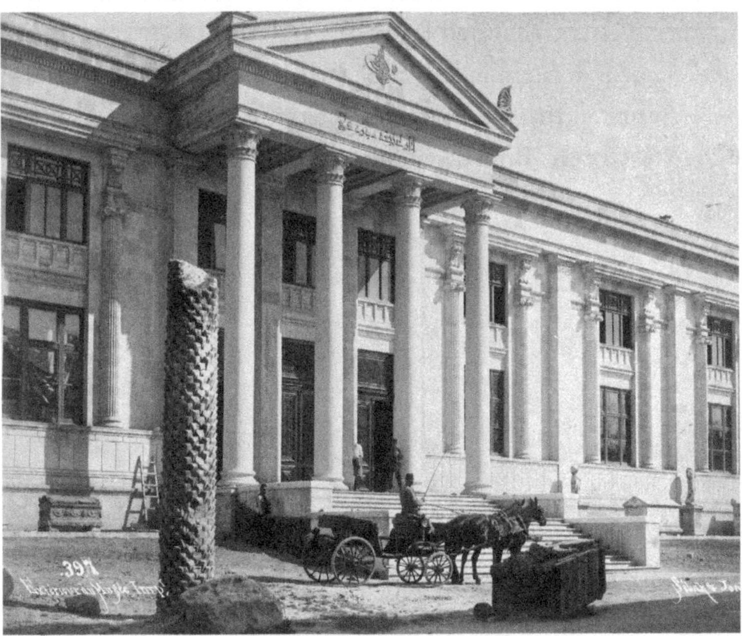

Graeco-Roman facade of the Imperial Ottoman Museum in Istanbul, 1900.

have been built in the style of Islamic palaces and mosques from the medieval era – replete with spellbinding geometric designs, pointed arches and domes – and would have privileged the collection and display of the material remains of the Umayyad and Abbasid Caliphates. And if that had been the case, there would have been little cause for competitive tension with Western collectors, for the two sides would have been hunting for entirely different types of ancient artefacts.

So the ultimate cause of non-Western resistance to the collecting activities of Western scholars is not that these Westerners were stealing the memories of their nation, for the most authentic and representative version of their 'nation' would have consisted chiefly of Islamic, Arabic and Persian elements – towards which Westerners evinced far less interest. Instead, the source of resistance lay in the fact that Western-educated Egyptians and Turks were coming to believe, under Western influence, that their proper 'national ancestors' were one and the same with the preferred civilizational ancestors of the Westerners. This elite adherence to Western cultural ideals

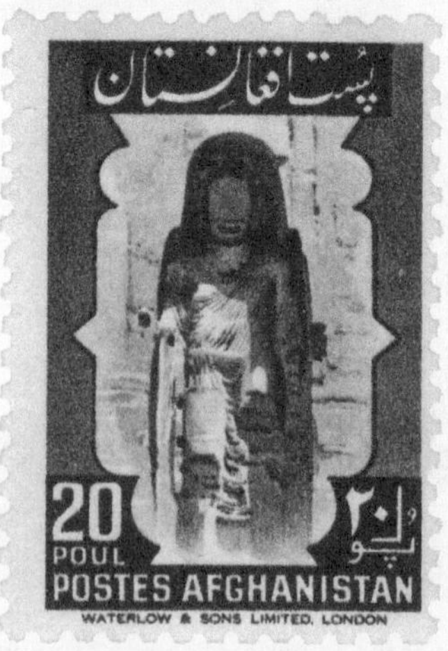

Afghanistan government stamp featuring Bamiyan Buddha, 1950s.

has created a deep and long-lasting rift with the majority of their subjects, who mostly saw in the crumbling pre-Islamic ruins of North Africa and the Middle East the just punishments meted out by Allah to stubborn pagans who wilfully defied His authority. This rift continues to plague the region today. Currency, stamps, street names, train station decor and government buildings – all sponsored by local elites – are filled with the iconography of the same pre-Islamic civilizations that Western collectors once coveted (and still do): the pharaonic past in Egypt, the Roman-influenced ruins of Palmyra in Syria, the Achaemenid ruins of Persepolis in Iran and the Bamiyan Buddhas in Afghanistan.

We can thus read the history of non-Western resistance to Western collectors as a product of competitive tensions that were shouldered almost entirely by a small sliver of Western-educated native elites in the face of the overwhelming indifference – and sometimes downright hostility – to this agenda by the majority of that country's lower-class citizens. In other words, Westernized Egyptian politicians and intellectuals, who were almost all educated in European institutions or tutored by Westernized Egyptian teachers at home, wanted to garner a larger slice of the archaeological pie for display in their Western-style museums, for the explicit purpose of teaching their Muslim subjects that their 'true' ancestors were the Western-approved pagan pharaohs, not the devout caliphs of the Umayyad or Abbasid empires. This is the somewhat ironic milieu within which non-Western resistance to Western scholars first crystallized: a desperate bid for cultural acceptance into the ranks of modernized Western countries, all at the expense, not the benefit, of the majority of people who comprised their 'nation'.

Viewed from this perspective, it should not surprise us to learn that most of these efforts by native elites to ape the facade of Western modernity through the curation of pre-Islamic ruins and antiquities failed to take root among the non-Western masses. This is why any threat to the modern Egyptian tourism industry – pandemics, terrorist attacks – are seen as significant blows to the economy, for the majority of people who will pay big bucks to climb the pyramids are not Egyptians, but rather foreign tourists. It is also why any time a radical Islamist group such as Da'esh or the Taliban seizes political power, one of the first things they do to try and shore up their populist credentials is to blow up archaeological emblems favoured not only by Western admirers, but more importantly by the Western-educated domestic admirers whom they had just managed to supplant in the halls of power: for instance, the ruins of Palmyra in Syria and the Bamiyan Buddhas in Afghanistan.

With this in mind, we can now finish the chronology of non-Western – but Western-educated – elite resistance to Western archaeologists. The reason we can only narrate this resistance as it relates to Western archaeologists is because scholars were a particularly visible and vulnerable target, and thus relatively easy to obstruct. But any attempts by non-Western elites to put an end to the collecting activities of any Western collector other than a scholar were destined to fail, because – as we have already seen – hardly anyone outside the halls of non-Western power and academia gave a fig about the fates of those sorts of antiquities favoured by Western collectors. This is why antiquities export laws enacted in Egypt failed to stem the flow of pharaonic artefacts outside the country. Marauding soldiers, of course, could never be stopped. And politicians – even those who had received a Western education – continued to gift away ancient artefacts whenever they deemed the expected diplomatic compensation to outweigh the cost of betraying their 'nation'. But most persistent of all were the dealers. They, too, were unstoppable because their activities were aided and abetted by nearly everyone in the country outside of the privileged Westernized ruling elite in the capital. In other words, there was simply no way for this tiny ruling elite to prevent the entire Egyptian nation from betraying itself.

Archaeologists alone could be stopped. Their excavations were large in scale, continued for weeks or months at a time, involved large investments of labour and resources from local communities, and were bound by the dictates of bureaucratic paperwork that humble scholars could not – try as they might – circumvent. One of the first Westerners to run afoul of new antiquities preservation laws in the Ottoman Empire was the German American businessman Heinrich Schliemann (1822–1890). A self-made tycoon who had struck it rich selling supplies to miners during the San Francisco gold rush and then as a military supplier to Russia during the Crimean War, Schliemann retired in 1864 at the ripe age of 42 and decided to devote his time and money to cultural pursuits. Over the course of the following decade, Schliemann financed an excavation to find the fabled city of Troy on the westernmost tip of Anatolia. The only problem was that he had paid absolutely no heed to newly enacted Ottoman laws regarding such excavations: applying for a firman to dig, purchasing the private land on which he dug, submitting his finds for official inspection, and allowing the authorities to divvy up his archaeological proceeds among several interested parties in accordance with a new practice known by its French name of *partage*.

Such laws only existed because the Ottomans now had a European-style museum in their capital, making it impossible for Westerners to claim that the Ottomans didn't cherish their history or have a place to preserve and study it. So when Schliemann found a spectacular collection of jewellery he dubbed 'Priam's Treasure' – named after the legendary king of Troy – he decided that, rather than submit it to

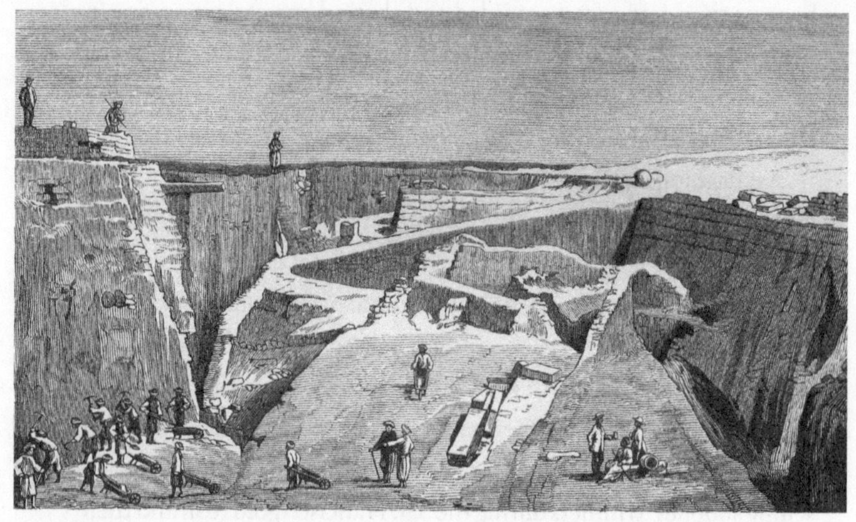

Heinrich Schliemann's excavations at Troy, 1873.

Turkish oversight and possibly lose it to *partage*, he would smuggle it out of the country. Once the Ottomans saw a picture of Priam's Treasure being worn by Schliemann's wife in a foreign newspaper, they demanded its immediate return. Instead, Schliemann 'donated' it to the Greek state, expecting to find a sympathetic reception there for his 'return' of ancient 'Greek' treasure. But the Greeks, faced with an Ottoman lawsuit in their own courts, moved to freeze Schliemann's assets and seize Priam's Treasure so that they could return it to its rightful legal owner: the Turks. Shocked by this move, Schliemann absconded once more with his find and eventually donated it to the Royal Museum of Berlin. There it remained until 1945, when the Soviet Red Army took Priam's Treasure as victor's spoils and deposited it in the Pushkin Museum of Fine Arts in Moscow.[31]

The most important lesson of the so-called Schliemann affair is that Ottoman laws concerning the disposition of newly unearthed antiquities were on the books by the late nineteenth century, and any

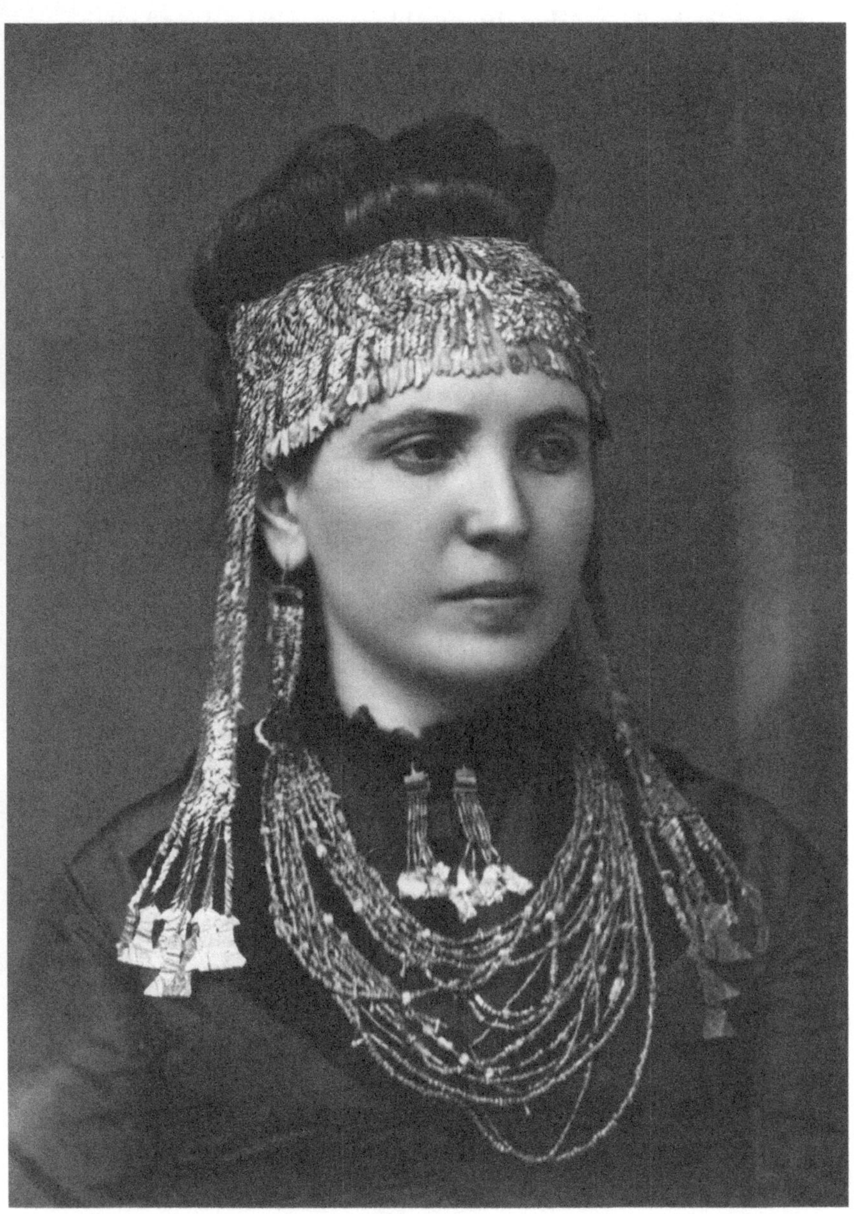

Priam's Treasure worn by Schliemann's wife, 1873.

foreigner who flouted those laws could expect swift legal retribution. As a result, Priam's Treasure is an excellent candidate for repatriation today, provided the Turks can convince Moscow to return it: after all, there is little doubt it was stolen in contravention of established laws of the day, and these were laws that the Ottomans actually tried to enforce. Schliemann's ability to evade these laws was unique: his considerable wealth precluded the need to affiliate with a higher institution of learning whose reputation might be sullied by his reprehensible behaviour. In that sense, he doesn't really fit the classic mould of those true scholars who had to beg from a well-endowed patron for every penny they spent in the field, and to whom they were responsible should an incident arise. Unlike Schliemann, most scholars who undertook excavations and expeditions would indeed have to abide by such new restrictions, no matter how they felt about them.

The golden age of obstruction, however, did not come until after the First World War. Prior to the signing of the Treaty of Versailles in 1919, Western-educated elites in non-Western lands had only chequered success in enforcing the Western-style antiquities laws they had passed, primarily because so few of their fellow citizens had any desire to enforce them. The locals were still willing to provide manual labour for wages, while customs officials could still be bribed. But the punitive measures imposed on the Ottoman Empire for having joined the wrong side of the war introduced an existential political crisis that gave Western-educated diplomats the excuse they needed to turn their particular version of the nation's past into a political reality, regardless of popular opposition. The Ottoman Empire itself was partitioned into a host of weak and ill-defined successor states, each of which needed to articulate a new cultural vision for its precarious national identity without delay. The Western ideal favoured by Western-educated native elites – that is, the material remains of the pre-Islamic past – quickly prevailed. Now the stakes had been raised so high that no one in a position of authority would dare to countenance the loss of any object portrayed as the priceless heritage of the newly conceived, and very artificial, nation.

The first act of obstruction inspired by these new principles took place immediately after the conclusion of the war in the freshly created successor state of Turkey. From 1910 to 1914, Princeton archaeologist Howard Butler excavated Greek, Lydian, Persian and Roman ruins at the site of Sardis, about 320 kilometres (200 mi.) southeast of Troy. When the war broke out, all American personnel withdrew and the artefacts were placed into local storage. Soon after the war, however, Greek forces invaded the port of İzmir and advanced inland. Turkish armies fought back, and the two sides came perilously close to lobbing artillery over the stored artefacts at Sardis. Butler's American financiers, who had close ties to the Metropolitan Museum, made the unilateral decision to remove 58 crates from storage and to place them into safekeeping in New York. The response of the Turks, who now depended on such artefacts to construct their new national identity in the pre-Islamic Western mould, was swift and decisive. In short, no new American excavation would ever be allowed to dig in Turkey again if the crates were not returned. The Americans capitulated, and the crates were returned.

It was that easy. When faced with recalcitrant scholars affiliated with august institutions of higher learning, all the host country had to do was say no. Of course, the Ottomans could have said the same thing to the Americans during the Schliemann affair forty years earlier, but instead decided to settle for a one-time cash payment of £2,000 and a promise not to do it again. That's because the Turks had not yet experienced an existential political crisis like the end of the First World War and the dismemberment of their empire; so exceptions could continue to be made in exchange for diplomatic goodwill, which was still valued higher than Priam's Treasure. But not any more. The artefacts from Sardis would now be used to construct a brand-new vision for a Western-influenced model of Turkey's new national identity that was entirely under the control of Turkish elites. With the future of the country now at stake in a way it had never been before, such antiquities became priceless in both name and fact. At least, they became so to anyone who subscribed to the Western preference for pre-Islamic artefacts, which included nearly all of the most wealthy and powerful people in Turkey – but few of its poor and downtrodden.

Another scholar who was easy to say no to was the British Egyptologist Howard Carter. In November 1922 Carter's team excavated the long-lost tomb of the boy pharaoh Tutankhamun, still virtually intact with more than 4,000 glittering treasures. Had Carter located the tomb during any one of his many previous excavations in the Valley of the Kings, it is almost certain that all the best artefacts would have ended up on the shelves of the British Museum in London and the Metropolitan Museum in New York. Instead, following a seemingly trivial dispute over who had the right to determine the daily guest list for tours of the tomb, the Egyptian government unilaterally decided to place a lock on the gate and take over ownership of the site. Once again, it was that easy. There was no acrimonious fistfight, shootout or diplomatic brawl over the ignominious removal of the most famous Egyptologist in history. Carter left Egypt in disgrace, only to return a year later once he had agreed to abide by all the new restrictions and oversight that the Western-educated Egyptian politicians in Cairo saw fit to impose on him.[32] Of course, they could have imposed the same restrictions on any other Western archaeologist over the past century simply by saying no, and then

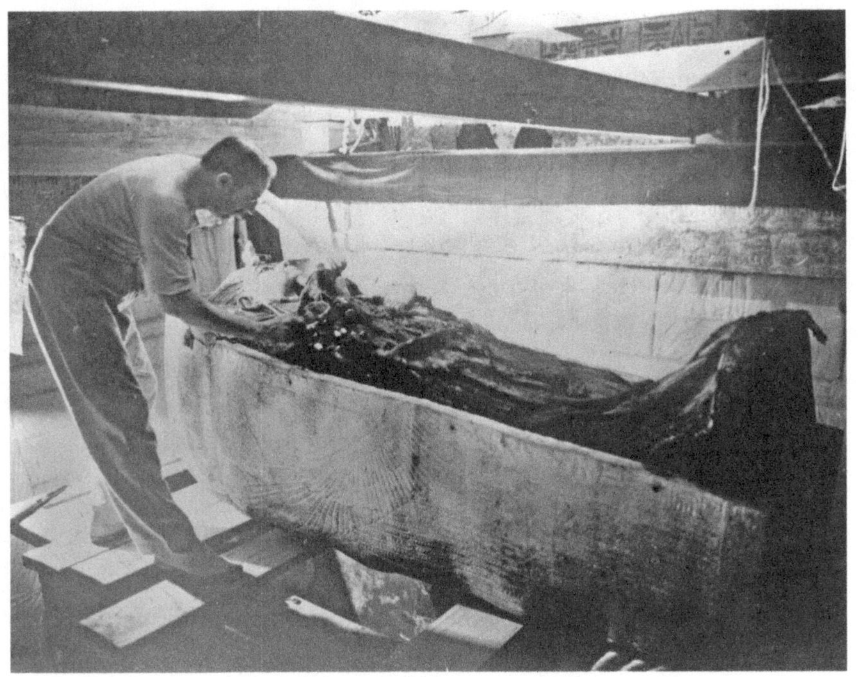

Howard Carter in Tutankhamun's tomb, 1926.

backing that sentiment up with a modest projection of bureaucratic authority. But until the existential crisis of the First World War and the rise to prominence of Western-educated politicians determined to construct a new Western-influenced historical genealogy for the Egyptian nation – kicking and screaming if need be – no one in Egypt felt strongly enough about their antiquities to do so.

In China, the narrative of obstruction also followed fast on the heels of the First World War, when the first generation of Western-educated Chinese intellectuals finally came of age and started to roar with principled disapproval at the post-war concessions granted by their Western wartime allies to Japan, all at the expense of China. Keep in mind just how easy it would have been to obstruct Stein during any one of his first three expeditions in the first two decades of the twentieth century had Chinese authorities wanted to do so: a stamp of rejection on his application for a Chinese passport, orders to local officials in Xinjiang to turn him away, and the publicization of economic or legal consequences for any commoners who signed up to work for him. The British consulate certainly would have criticized the Chinese lack of cooperation with Stein as 'unscientific' and 'backward', but these were words, not bullets, and the Chinese knew that Westerners would continue to denigrate them privately behind their backs regardless.

But now, all the conditions were in place to say no to men like Stein – and mean it. Western-educated intellectuals held high posts in government and the old empire had been overthrown. So Westernized Chinese politicians needed to construct a new collective national identity based on the ruins of antiquity, and Western scholars were the only target they could attack successfully without broad-based support from the masses (who continue to supply dealers to this day). The first casualty was Harvard art historian Langdon Warner, who undertook an expedition to the Mogao Grottoes near Dunhuang in 1925. When a Western-educated intellectual named William Hung – his English name instantly betrays his educational pedigree – heard that Warner had cut out Buddhist murals from the cave walls on a prior expedition a few years earlier, he alerted the Ministry of Education. The ministry in turn sent out telegrams to all officials along Warner's route to make sure he did not remove anything from their jurisdictions. And it worked – nothing more than a simple telegram was required to obstruct the high and mighty Westerners.

Stein met with a similar fate on his fourth and final expedition to Xinjiang in 1930. Well aware of Warner's fate just five years earlier,

Stein first wrote ahead to his friends among the Uyghurs and Chinese politicians of old to see if they subscribed to the new nationalist platform of coastal intellectuals or not. When they uniformly expressed support for another expedition – for none of them were Western-educated – he decided to try his luck. Incredibly, the Ministry of Foreign Affairs in Nanjing approved his application for another expedition, still hoping to curry diplomatic favour with the British government as well as Harvard University, which funded most of Stein's expedition. But a group of Western-educated young intellectuals in Beijing, who had formed a Commission for the Preservation of Antiquities, decided to mount a public relations campaign against Stein and all his backers – both foreign and domestic – once they caught wind of his expedition. Again it worked: Chiang Kai-shek's new government in Nanjing, terrified of losing the vocal support of nationalist scholars who now claimed to speak on behalf of the newly reimagined Chinese nation, caved to their demands and promptly cancelled Stein's passport. Stein departed from Xinjiang in disgrace, and the age of Western expeditions in China was over.[33]

It is worth noting that in every single case where Western archaeologists were kicked out of a source country, the country that put an end to their excavations was much smaller and weaker than its predecessors who had regularly approved and supported such excavations prior to the First World War. Turkey was a fraction of the size of the Ottoman Empire and was engaged in a bloody war with Greece when they clamped down on the Sardis artefacts. Egypt no longer had the backing of the Ottoman sultan when it showed Carter the exit door. And China was at the very nadir of its modern political and economic power when its politicians finally decided to obstruct Warner and Stein – in fact, three-quarters of the country was still ruled by autonomous warlords and colonial concessions were at their height.

It is thus emphatically not the case that Western scholars were obstructed once the natives finally got tired of colonial oppression and decided to stand up for themselves, as is so often suggested in facile representations of these pivotal events. It is much more accurate to say that Western archaeologists came to dig in foreign lands when native authorities said yes, and they ceased to dig in foreign lands when native authorities said no. The fact that scholars were so easy to obstruct once the authorities decided to say no underscores just how complicit those authorities had once been during the heyday of Western excavations, for it took no great show of military force or political bombast to stop a tenured professor of history in his tracks. A lock on a gate, a stamp of rejection or a promise never to welcome another expedition from that scholar's home country was all it took. And when rejection finally did come, it was not because the natives suddenly woke up to the fact that their memories were being stolen by Western imperialists. It came about because Western scholars had managed to convince native elites that these antiquities were priceless emblems of the nations or empires that acquired them, and that the only respectable way for modern, enlightened citizens of these nations or empires to interact with such priceless objects was by putting them in a museum – their museum, not just any museum – for the sake of science, preservation and education. In that sense, Western scholars dug their own archaeological grave.

CONCLUSION

If you ever happen to find yourself on the island of Taiwan, you might consider taking a few hours to pay a visit to the Chimei Museum. Located in the southern city of Tainan, the Chimei Museum was founded in 1992 and moved into its current building in 2014 – and what a building it is! As visitors approach the white colonnaded portico of the main facade, they could be forgiven for thinking they were in any number of major Western cities whose public monuments and museums burst forth in faux Graeco-Roman architecture. The main promenade to the entrance of the Chimei Museum is lined on either side with rows of classical statues, bleach white under the hot tropical sun, and culminating in a water fountain filled with dramatic sculptures of Greek gods pulled on a chariot by a team of robust horses. The scene inside the museum is no less startling. There is a hall for Western fine arts from the thirteenth to the twentieth century, a Rodin Gallery, musical instrument displays featuring rare violins, its own Ancient Greco-Roman Sculpture Hall, and an Arms and Armour exhibit complete with a life-size reconstruction of a jousting tournament from medieval Europe.

According to the popular critique of museums fashionable in our own day and age, the artefacts displayed inside the Chimei Museum

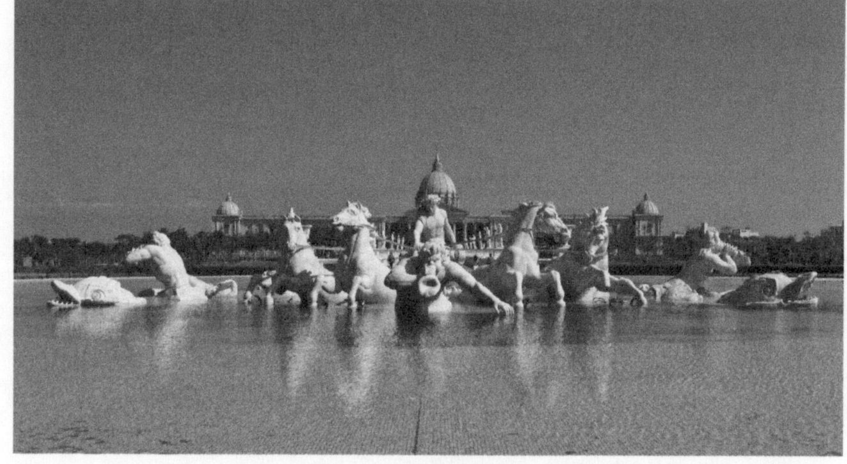

The Chimei Museum in Tainan, Taiwan.

must be the result of imperialist plunder. After all, to walk into a museum today is to walk into a vast, carefully curated crime scene in which only the most enlightened and progressive of visitors can see the blood and oppression slathered across every marble surface. But the Chimei Museum serves as a reminder that appearances can be deceptive. The idea that its Western collections might be seen as a reflection of 'Taiwanese imperialism' in Western lands is downright absurd. On the contrary, anyone who walks into the Palace Museum at the Forbidden City in Beijing – or any other museum in China – will probably assume that everything on display was obtained peacefully and legitimately. After all, it is a Chinese museum displaying Chinese works of art. But such assumptions would be wrong: after 1949 the Chinese Communist Party regularly seized private collections from Chinese owners without their consent and without any compensation, before integrating their contents into museum collections without any acknowledgement of their morally dubious provenance.[1]

So museum collections are not always as they appear on first glance. A Chinese museum filled with only Chinese artefacts, run by Chinese curators and catering largely to Chinese visitors can be deeply implicated in blatant theft, while a Taiwanese museum awash in the material trappings and collections of the classical West can be assembled in recent decades without any morally suspect acquisition methods whatsoever. After all, Taiwan is about as politically weak as a state can be: only 12 out of 193 United Nations member states maintain formal diplomatic relations with this tiny island nation. And yet one of its richest citizens, the successful Taiwanese businessman Wen-Long Shi, somehow managed to accumulate thousands of top-notch works of art from a culturally alien society without the benefit of a single ounce of imperialist power at his disposal.

Most of us are surprised by this revelation, but we shouldn't be. As we have seen over the course of this book, there were always ways to assemble a culturally alien collection of art that did not transgress the values and cultural expectations of the day nor depend on the application of imperialist force. The problem is that we now insist on retroactively applying our own set of moral principles – unique to our own era – backwards in time to serve as an ahistorical moral barometer for the actions of long-dead historical figures who can no longer speak in their own defence. These moral principles, however, arose in a certain place and time and only among a certain group of people – that is, among Western-educated elites in non-Western countries who were traumatized by the political consequences of the First World War. As a result they resorted to using the Western valuation of the 'priceless' material remains of the past to construct a new national identity that the vast majority of their impoverished and poorly educated compatriots had never recognized or embraced. This was also true, as we saw in the case of the Chinese officials who interacted with Aurel Stein and Paul Pelliot at the dawn of the twentieth century, of those wealthy native elites who had received an 'old school' cosmopolitan education in which the abstract 'nation' played almost no role. They, too, resisted the idea that such things could serve as priceless symbols of political legitimacy that precluded the possibility of trading them away in the interests of science, friendship or profit.

Unfortunately, this is the misleading discourse with which we are stuck today. Because the act of putting an object into a museum confers upon that object a new priceless valuation – that is, once accessioned to a museum it can never be sold again – the casual observer simply assumes that it must have been stolen or plundered from its original owners. For who would have ever willingly countenanced the removal of anything deemed priceless to their community? As a result, the discourse of cultural restitution builds upon the assumption that everything in a museum once had a more legitimate owner: if not a hapless flesh-and-blood individual who was bamboozled out of his priceless possession by cunning Westerners, then the eternal nation from under whose sacred soil a greedy Western archaeologist removed it via secrecy, deceit and force. But as we have seen throughout this book, neither assumption is supported by historical evidence. Private owners willingly and voluntarily sold their artistic wares to foreigners, and almost no one believed in the sovereignty of the abstract 'nation': if the earth yielded up its treasures, then that treasure belonged to whoever dug it up (or whoever paid to have it dug up on their behalf). And nothing was priceless: everything could be sold, traded, bequeathed or gifted away anytime the perceived value of what was being received exceeded the perceived value of what was being lost. The key word here is 'perceive': a subjective action wherein value is determined by contemporary norms of historical actors, not by the norms of future critics pursuing moral agendas undreamt of by the parties involved in the original transaction.

Though there were exceptions, in the vast majority of cases in which antiquities crossed cultural boundaries en route to a Western museum, a large number of people drawn from nearly all walks of life in the source country knew what was being removed, did not pass a negative moral judgement upon that removal and – perhaps most importantly – were deeply complicit in the process of removal. To say that they were complicit is not to levy a negative judgement on them today, for their historical complicity is both easy to understand and sympathize with. As we have seen, native elites were happy to trade away antiquities for diplomatic, political or social capital, while the native poor were eager to take their fair market share of the economic capital on tap. Viewed from the perspective of impoverished illiterate Egyptian *fellahin* or Chinese peasants, this was a form of harmless wealth redistribution. Viewed from the historian's perspective, we might refer to such exchanges as the compensations of cooperation. With the sole exception of military plunder, the only victims of the antiquities trade – be they carried out by native or Western diplomats, dealers or scholars – were intellectual abstractions such as the artificial nation or the pretensions of science.

And yet even this judgement is too harsh. After all, few museums anywhere in the world are hurting for lack of supply, and scholars have far more material to subject to careful scientific scrutiny than they have actual time and resources to devote to such study. For instance, the permanent collection of the National Palace Museum in Taiwan, which holds the best objects taken from the Forbidden City in the 1930s, contains nearly 700,000 items in its catalogue. With only enough display space and curators to put about 3,000 of these items on display at any given time, it will take more than two hundred complete rotations of its display cases to exhibit the entire collection. In other words, no person currently alive will ever be able to view everything the National Palace Museum has within a single lifetime – or perhaps even two or three. Its counterpart in Beijing, the Palace Museum, holds more than twice that number of objects, many of which were forcibly seized from private Chinese owners by the Communist Party after 1949 – who among the critics of cultural theft are calling for their return to their 'rightful' owners?

Astute readers will notice that this book has devoted scant attention to the sort of moral arguments that are usually put forth by defenders of Western museums, a group that can now be considered an endangered species. Such defences often suggest that artefacts would have been destroyed sooner or later if not taken abroad by Western collectors, and that far more objects have been preserved in the West than would have otherwise occurred if left to the tender mercies of their original host countries. Another approach that has gained some traction is to try and rebrand and reimagine the Western 'imperial museum' (a symbol of empire) as an 'encyclopaedic museum' (a symbol of cosmopolitanism) that privileges no single culture or people but rather celebrates all civilizations that have ever existed more or less equally alongside one another. Last but not least are claims that great works of art should be placed where the greatest number of people can view them: thus the British Museum in London, which welcomes around 6 million visitors per year, is a more appropriate home for the Benin Bronzes than the Nigerian National Museum in Lagos, which sees only a fraction of such tourist traffic.

All of these arguments merely lead to more counter-arguments, all of which are based on present-day agendas and values: objects in Western museums have also been damaged by various means, so the critics will say, while the idea of the encyclopaedic museum is merely a rhetorical smokescreen for an imperialist museum. And the Nigerian National Museum in Lagos may very well receive a much larger number of visitors if they had their most spectacular 'stolen' art on display. Rather than continue to engage such irresolvable and circular debates, I have endeavoured to take a different approach: the historian's approach. The job of a historian is to reconstruct the past as much possible so that we can understand why things happened the way they did. The job of the historian is *not* to wish the past were different and to look only for the seeds of politically correct change that support the activist agendas of our own day and age. Instead, the historian is charged with explaining why people who were just as intelligent, observant and rational as we are today acted in a manner that we find wholly inexplicable or perhaps even reprehensible. And unless we are prepared to characterize every single non-Westerner who came into contact with a Western collector as traitorous, corrupt, venal or helpless, then we need to come up with a better, more nuanced depiction of how Western museums got their treasures.

All of the case studies and evidence presented in the preceding chapters have pointed to a simple conclusion. In short, the reason Westerners could remove so much art and antiquities from foreign lands was because they had ample, enthusiastic assistance from nearly everyone in those lands, almost none of whom thought that what they or the Westerner was doing was immoral. The idea that every single artefact in a Western museum required the use of imperialist force and deception in order to acquire it defies basic common sense. Western governments in general had very little appetite for military expenditures and casualties in distant lands, and none whatsoever for the acquisition and transport of antiquities. It is time to stop telling the story of Western collectors in non-Western lands as if it unfolded out of the pages of a comic book, where arrogant, half-clothed rogues shot their way through exotic lands, a golden idol in one hand and the rungs of a helicopter in the other, desperately clinging on for dear life just out of reach of a lynch mob. Hostile locals were rare; and if they did happen to be hostile, in all likelihood it had nothing to do with tensions over who owned the ancient bas-reliefs the archaeologist was collecting, but rather disputes over bad camp food or a reluctance to confront desert jinns. And the lands weren't exotic: native elites fully embraced the Western scientific ethos and the impoverished commoners were just as eager as their destitute brethren elsewhere to earn a living wage through an honest day's work. And, perhaps most importantly, outside of a military expedition, guns were a rare sight – unless, of course, an antelope needed to be shot for dinner.

History demands that a much less dramatic and less acrimonious story be told. After all, the scholars got their science, dealers got their profits, peasants got their wages and rewards, Western curators got their collections, and, once they wanted them, non-Western curators got their collections as well. Again, the historical evidence canvassed in this book merely confirms what common sense could have told us long ago: if any one of these groups did not receive something that they deemed more valuable in exchange for something they deemed less valuable, Western collectors would not have been able to take away anything other than what their soldiers might stumble upon during a military looting expedition. History is a living will, and the job of a historian is to treat that will as the embodiment of a rational and considered thought process from people who knew far better than we do the moral parameters of their day.

As the historical beneficiaries of these wills, we may not like what we see. But do we have the right to tell our ancestors what they should have thought and done, and blame them for acting in a way that did not accord with the unanticipated mores of a century or two hence? In order to explain how museums got their treasures, we have found it necessary to look beyond Western collectors and identify the many native historical figures who willingly and enthusiastically helped them remove these treasures from their lands. It is time to stop dismissing these helping hands as a mere handful of imperialist dupes or collaborators who were forced to make the best of a bad situation. Such a judgement does not reflect the historical evidence and merely serves to further silence the voices of non-Western historical actors. On the contrary, those non-Westerners who condoned the removal of art and antiquities to Western lands stood firmly in the majority, while those who opposed it were a distinct minority, if they even existed at all. Had this balance been reversed, the only thing you would find inside a Western museum today would be the occasional spoils of overt military plunder – a poor show indeed. Nearly everything else arrived as an unobjectionable and widely embraced result of what the historian can only describe as the compensations of cooperation.

not second-rate by the [illegible] of a century or two [illegible]. In order to explain how museums got their treasures, we have found it necessary to look beyond the collections and identify the many native historical figures who willingly and enthusiastically helped them remove their treasures from their lands. It is time to stop dismissing these helping hands as a mere handful of unprincipled dupes or collaborators who were forced to make the best of a bad situation. Such a judgement does not reflect the historical evidence and merely serves to further silence the [illegible] of non-Western historical actors. On the contrary, those non-Westerners who condoned the removal of art and antiquities to Western lands stood firmly in the majority, while those who opposed it were a distinct minority, if they even existed at all. Had this balance been reversed, the only thing you would find inside a Western museum today would be the occasional spoils of war, pillage or plunder – a poor show indeed. Nearly everything we admire at [illegible] museums was widely embraced by people at the time, and historians can only distort this by the [illegible] of [illegible].

REFERENCES

INTRODUCTION

1 Dan Hicks, *The Brutish Museums: The Benin Bronzes, Colonial Violence and Cultural Restitution* (London, 2020), p. xiii.

2 My thanks to Dallas Flynt for sharing a recording of John Oliver's monologue with me.

3 Hicks, *The Brutish Museums*, p. 243.

4 Fredrik Hagen and Kim Ryholt, *The Antiquities Trade in Egypt, 1880–1930: The H. O. Lange Papers* (Copenhagen, 2016), p. 8.

1 PRESENTS AND PLUNDER

1 Jo Anne Van Tilburg, *Remote Possibilities: Hoa Hakananai'a and* HMS *'Topaze' on Rapa Nui* (London, 2006), p. 28.

2 Ibid., pp. 28–30.

3 Ibid., p. 37.

4 Ibid., p. 51.

5 William St Clair, *Lord Elgin and the Marbles: The Controversial History of the Parthenon Sculptures* (Oxford, 1998), p. 92.

6 For the most complete account of Elgin's removal of the Parthenon sculptures, see ibid., pp. 43–118.

7 Elliott Colla, *Conflicted Antiquities: Egyptology, Egyptomania, Egyptian Modernity* (Durham, NC, 2007), pp. 30–31.

8 In addition to Colla's study cited above, one of the most accessible and detailed accounts of Belzoni's time in Egypt is Ivor Noël Hume, *Belzoni: The Giant Archaeologists Love to Hate* (Charlottesville, VA, 2011).

9 Giovanni Belzoni, *Narrative of the Operations and Recent Discoveries within the Pyramids, Temples, Tombs, and Excavations, in Egypt and*

Nubia and of a Journey to the Coast of the Red Sea, in Search of the Ancient Berenice; and Another to the Oasis of Jupiter Ammon (London, 1822), pp. 133 and 135.

10 Ibid., p. 135.

11 Hume, *Belzoni*, p. 211.

12 See 'A Tang Dynasty Stele Given by a Chinese Diplomat to the Field Museum in 1907', Chinese American Museum of Chicago, www.ccamuseum.org, 22 June 2023.

13 Stein Papers, Bodleian Library, Oxford University, MS 199, 27 May 1907, field diary entry.

14 Wang Shu'nan, *Xinjiang fang gu lu* [Record of antiquities in Xinjiang] (n.p., 1911), p. 20.

15 Wu Haokun and Pan You, *Zhongguo jiaguxue shi* [A history of the study of oracle bones in China] (Shanghai, 1991), pp. 11–12.

16 Justin M. Jacobs, *The Compensations of Plunder: How China Lost Its Treasures* (Chicago, IL, 2020), pp. 84–5.

17 Ping Foong, 'Serendipity in Seattle: An Early Dispersal Dunhuang Manuscript from the Library Cave', *Silk Roads Archaeology and Heritage*, forthcoming. The following account of the manuscript's journey is also informed by personal communication with Dr Foong.

18 David Allen, *How Mechanics Shaped the Modern World* (Cham, 2014), pp. 26–7; and Margaret Miles, *Art as Plunder: The Ancient Origins of Debate about Cultural Property* (Cambridge, 2008), p. 247.

19 Theresa Machemer, 'Egypt Defies Archaeologists' Protests by Relocating Four Ancient Sphinxes', *Smithsonian Magazine*, 11 May 2020.

20 Miles, *Art as Plunder*, p. 16.

21 Erin L. Thompson, *Possession: The Curious History of Private Collectors from Antiquity to the Present* (New Haven, CT, 2016), p. 8.

22 Miles, *Art as Plunder*, p. 19.

23 Ibid., p. 48.

24 Shao-yun Yang, 'Letting the Troops Loose: Pillages, Massacres, and Enslavement in Early Tang Warfare', *Journal of Chinese Military History*, VI/1 (July 2017), pp. 1–52.

25 Patricia Buckley Ebrey, *Accumulating Culture: The Collections of Emperor Huizong* (Seattle, WA, 2008), pp. 342–54.

26 Yang, 'Letting the Troops Loose'.

27 Tansen Sen, 'Zheng He's Military Interventions in South Asia, 1405–1433', *China and Asia*, I (2019), pp. 158–91.
28 St Clair, *Lord Elgin and the Marbles*, p. 100.
29 Donald Malcolm Reid, *Whose Pharaohs? Archaeology, Museums, and Egyptian National Identity from Napoleon to World War I* (Berkeley, CA, 2002), p. 32.
30 Matthew James Van Duyn, 'Remembering Imperialism in China: British and Chinese Representations of the Destruction of the Yuan Ming Yuan', Wesleyan College honours thesis, 2009, p. 116.
31 Ibid., pp. 28, 60, 62.
32 James L. Hevia, 'Looting and Its Discontents: Moral Discourse and the Plunder of Beijing, 1900–1901', in *The Boxers, China and the World*, ed. Robert A. Bickers and R. G. Tiedemann (Lanham, MD, 2007), p. 102.
33 Mao Cheng's poem is reprinted with an English translation in Geremie Barmé, 'The Garden of Perfect Brightness, a Life in Ruins', George Ernest Morrison Lecture in Ethnology, The Australian National University, Canberra, 1996, p. 137. The present translation, however, is my own.
34 Guolong Lai, 'The Emergence of "Cultural Heritage" in Modern China: A Historical and Legal Perspective', in *Reconsidering Cultural Heritage in East Asia*, ed. Akira Matsuda and Luisa E. Mengoni (London, 2016), p. 48.
35 Nicole T. C. Chiang, *Emperor Qianlong's Hidden Treasures: Reconsidering the Collection of the Qing Imperial Household* (Hong Kong, 2019), pp. 16, 26.
36 Letter from 25 October 1860, quoted in Theodore Walrond, ed., *Letters and Journals of James, Eighth Earl of Elgin* (London, 1872).
37 Adam Brookes, *Fragile Cargo: The World War II Race to Save the Treasures of China's Forbidden City* (New York, 2023).

2 DEALERS

1 Justin M. Jacobs, *Indiana Jones in History: From Pompeii to the Moon* (n.p., 2017), p. 237.
2 For instance, the Golden Idol found in the jungles of Peru is later revealed to have been a commission for the fictional National Museum in Washington, DC; the search for the Ark of the Covenant was

commissioned by U.S. 'Army Intelligence', who are said to be 'ready to pay handsomely'; the Urn of Nurhaci was a private commission from the Shanghai crime-lord Lao Che, who professed his excitement at getting his hands on the ashes of his 'sacred ancestor'; and the search for the Holy Grail was a private commission from the wealthy American businessman Walter Donovan – the only reason Jones undertakes this last mission is because he wants to find his missing father, who disappeared while searching for the Grail.

3 Fredrik Hagen and Kim Ryholt, *The Antiquities Trade in Egypt, 1880–1930: The H. O. Lange Papers* (Copenhagen, 2016), p. 43.

4 Qiang Yong quoted in Nicole T. C. Chiang, *Emperor Qianlong's Hidden Treasures: Reconsidering the Collection of the Qing Imperial Household* (Hong Kong, 2019), p. 124.

5 Erin L. Thompson, *Possession: The Curious History of Private Collectors from Antiquity to the Present* (New Haven, CT, 2016), p. 160.

6 Patricia Buckley Ebrey, *Accumulating Culture: The Collections of Emperor Huizong* (Seattle, WA, 2008), p. 109.

7 Hagen and Ryholt, *The Antiquities Trade in Egypt*, pp. 65, 73.

8 Ibid., pp. 29, 147.

9 Ibid., p. 31.

10 For the full, annotated list of dealers, see Hagen and Ryholt, *The Antiquities Trade in Egypt*, pp. 183–274. The American gynaecologist-turned-dealer was Dr David Leslie Askren (1875–1939).

11 Hagen and Ryholt, *The Antiquities Trade in Egypt*, pp. 43, 47–9.

12 Ibid., pp. 131, 119.

13 Ibid., p. 57.

14 See, for instance, David Matsuda, 'The Ethics of Archaeology, Subsistence Digging, and Artifact Looting in Latin America', *International Journal of Cultural Property*, VII/1 (January 1998), pp. 87–97.

15 Hagen and Ryholt, *The Antiquities Trade in Egypt*, pp. 26–7.

16 Ibid., p. 152. Despite all these preparations, the prince did not embark on his scheduled trip to Egypt.

17 Ibid., pp. 33–4.

18 Stein Papers, Bodleian Library, Oxford University, MS 199, 28 May 1907.

19 Hagen and Ryholt, *The Antiquities Trade in Egypt*, p. 49.

20 Ibid., pp. 146, 190.

21 The story was originally printed in *Scribner's Magazine*, but is also reprinted in full in Hagen and Ryholt, *The Antiquities Trade in Egypt*, pp. 291–5.

22 Chen Zhongyuan, *Guwan tan jiuwen* [Recollections about the antiquities trade] (Beijing, 1996), p. 14.

23 Ibid., pp. 11–16.

24 Los Angeles County Museum of Art and Percival David Foundation of Chinese Art, *Imperial Taste: Chinese Ceramics from the Percival David Foundation* (San Francisco, CA, 1989), p. 10; and Chen, *Guwan tan jiuwen*, pp. 91–3.

25 Nancy Shatzman Steinhardt, *Chinese Architecture: A History* (Princeton, NJ, 2019), p. 97.

26 Alice Y. Tseng, *The Imperial Museums of Meiji Japan: Architecture and the Art of the Nation* (Seattle, WA, 2008), pp. 146–50; Bénédicte Savoy et al., eds, *Acquiring Cultures: Histories of World Art on Western Markets* (Berlin, 2018), pp. 211–12; and the Metropolitan Museum of Art, 'Buddha of Medicine Bhaishajyaguru (Yaoshi fo)', Gallery 206, www.metmuseum.org, 22 June 2023.

27 Sebastian Smee and Peggy McGlone, 'A Baltimore Museum Tried to Raise Money by Selling Three Pricey Artworks. It Backfired Stupendously', *Washington Post*, 6 December 2020; and Xie Xiaozhong [Xie Bin], *Xinjiang youji* [A record of travels in Xinjiang] [1923] (Lanzhou, 2002), p. 246.

28 Chen, *Guwan tan jiuwen*, pp. 21–5.

29 Ibid., pp. 105–10.

30 Ibid., p. 130.

31 Ibid., p. 174.

32 Ian Johnson, 'How a Chu Silk Manuscript Ended Up in Washington', *New York Times*, 8 June 2018.

33 All known documentation concerning Cai's intention to sell the Chu Silk Manuscript with the help of Cox can be found in Ling Li, *The Chu Silk Manuscripts from Zidanku, Changsha (Hunan Province)*, vol. I: *Discovery and Transmission*, trans. Lothar von Falkenhausen (Hong Kong, 2020). In letters written by Cai during 1946–7, he describes the manuscripts as belonging 'to me and to the firm of Mr. Ye [Shuchong]' (p. 125), the Shanghai dealer with links to New York. Cai's later claim

that he had only reluctantly lent the manuscript to Cox for scanning, not for resale, and that Cox then subsequently absconded with it, is not mentioned for the first time until 1974 (pp. 118–19). All correspondence from the late 1940s discusses the manuscript in plain business terms, along with mention of other antiquities that Cai hoped to sell to Cox in Shanghai.

34 The only scholarly biography of Loo thus far is in French. See Géraldine Lenain, *Monsieur Loo: Le Roman d'un marchand d'art asiatique* (Arles, 2013). My narration of Loo's career derives from the Chinese translation of the French edition: Luo-la (Géraldine Lenain), *Lu Qinzhai zhuan* [Biography of Lu Qinzhai], trans. Bian Wanyu (Xianggang, 2013).

35 Huang Wenbi, *Huang Wenbi Meng Xin kaocha riji: 1927–1930* [The diary of Huang Wenbi during a survey of Mongolia and Xinjiang: 1927–1930] (Beijing, 1990), p. 279.

36 On the removal of Buddhist statuary and reliefs from the Longmen Grottoes, see Dong Wang, *Longmen's Stone Buddhas and Cultural Heritage: When Antiquity Met Modernity in China* (Lanham, MD, 2020), pp. 181–90; and Karl E. Meyer and Shareen Blair Brysac, *The China Collectors: America's Century-Long Hunt for Asian Art Treasures* (New York, 2015), pp. 81–101.

37 Meyer and Brysac, *The China Collectors*, p. 86.

38 Wang, *Longmen's Stone Buddhas and Cultural Heritage*, pp. 187–8.

39 Tracey L.-D. Lu, *Museums in China: Power, Politics, and Identities* (London, 2014), pp. 90–91.

40 Meyer and Brysac, *The China Collectors*, p. 111.

41 Ibid., p. 112.

42 Lara Jaishree Netting, *A Perpetual Fire: John C. Ferguson and His Quest for Chinese Art and Culture* (Hong Kong, 2013), pp. 94–5.

43 Luo-la (Lenain), *Lu Qinzhai zhuan*, pp. 167–9.

44 C. T. Loo, *An Exhibition of Chinese Stone Sculptures* (New York, 1940), preface.

45 Chen, *Guwan tan jiuwen*, pp. 121–5.

3 EXCAVATIONS AND EXPEDITIONS

1 Shirley M. Mueller, 'Charles Lang Freer and C. T. Loo, Mentor and Mentee: Cultural Clashes and Neuropsychological Insights', in *Ceramics in America*, ed. Robert Hunter (Milwaukee, WI, 2015), p. 58.
2 Yiyou Wang, 'The Loouvre from China: A Critical Study of C. T. Loo and the Framing of Chinese Art in the United States, 1915–1950', PhD dissertation, Ohio University, November 2007, p. 121.
3 Justin M. Jacobs, *The Compensations of Plunder: How China Lost Its Treasures* (Chicago, IL, 2020), p. 176.
4 Ibid., p. 43.
5 Erin L. Thompson, *Possession: The Curious History of Private Collectors from Antiquity to the Present* (New Haven, CT, 2016); and Justin M. Jacobs, 'An Analysis of Modern Chinese Colophons on the Dunhuang Manuscripts', *The Silk Road*, XVII (2019), pp. 74–89.
6 Christopher Charles Parslow, *Rediscovering Antiquity: Karl Weber and the Excavation of Herculaneum, Pompeii, and Stabiae* (Cambridge, 1995), pp. 147, 211.
7 Donald Malcolm Reid, *Whose Pharaohs? Archaeology, Museums, and Egyptian National Identity from Napoleon to World War I* (Berkeley, CA, 2002), p. 61.
8 Margaret S. Drower, ed., *Letters from the Desert: The Correspondence of Flinders and Hilda Petrie* (Oxford, 2004), p. 2.
9 Stephen Quirke, *Hidden Hands: Egyptian Workforces in Petrie Excavation Archives, 1880–1924* (London, 2010), pp. 59, 101, 198–270.
10 Eric Schluessel, 'A Poem of Praise for the Expedition, by Obulmahdi of Karakhoja', draft translation, reprinted with permission. The original poem, in Arabic script with a German translation, was published in Albert von Le Coq, *Sprichwörter und Lieder aus der Gegend von Turfan mit einer dort aufgenommenen Wörterliste* (Leipzig and Berlin, 1911), pp. 68–78.
11 Jacobs, *The Compensations of Plunder*, pp. 67–8.
12 Paul Pelliot, *Carnets de route, 1906–1908* (Paris, 2008), pp. 87, 364. All English translations from Paul Pelliot's diary and letters in French were completed by Shilah Marks.

13 Papers of Ellsworth Huntington, Manuscripts and Archives, Yale University Library, Series 1, box 6, folder 65, 14 March 1906.

14 Stein Papers, Bodleian Library, Oxford University, MS 37, 14 May 1907; Stein Papers, Bodleian Library, Oxford University, MS 107, 17 September 1922; and Wang Jiqing, 'Jiang Xiaowan wannian shiji kaoshi' [An analysis of events in the later years of Jiang Xiaowan], *Dunhuangxue jikan*, III (2013), pp. 153–63.

15 Pelliot, *Carnets de route*, p. 62; and Stein Papers, Bodleian Library, Oxford University, MS 193, 1 April 1901.

16 Jacobs, *The Compensations of Plunder*, pp. 75–81, 41.

17 Pelliot, *Carnets de route*, pp. 139, 85, 20; and Stein Papers, Bodleian Library, Oxford University, MS 198, 18 February 1907.

18 Zhongguo Xinjiang Weiwuer zizhiqu dang'an guan and Riben fojiao daxue Niya yizhi xueshu yanjiu jigou, eds, *Jindai waiguo tanxianjia Xinjiang kaogu dang'an shiliao* [Archival materials concerning the archaeological expeditions of foreign explorers in modern Xinjiang] (Wulumuqi, 2001), pp. 108–9.

19 For the original Chinese translation of Stein's *Preliminary Report on a Journey of Archaeological and Topographical Exploration in Chinese Turkestan* (1901), see 'You Hua fanggu ji' [A record of archaeological exploration in China], in *Guojia tushuguan cang guji zhenben youji congkan* [Old and rare travel accounts in the collection of the National Library of China], ed. Liu Jiaping and Zhou Jiming, vol. V (Beijing, 2003), pp. 2423–524. For an English translation and additional insightful commentary, see Imre Galambos, 'A Forgotten Chinese Translation of the Preliminary Report of Aurel Stein's First Expedition', in *Dunhuang Studies: Prospects and Problems for the Coming Second Century of Research*, ed. Irina Popova and Liu Yi (St Petersburg, 2012), pp. 55–8. I have used Galambos's translation for the English excerpts included here.

20 All of the Chinese-language correspondence sent from Chinese officials to Stein can be found in Stein Papers, Bodleian Library, Oxford University, MS 341–2. All English translations are my own, with the exception of the letter from Dai Chengmo, which was translated with the generous assistance of Ely Finch.

21 *Notes et manuscrits de Paul Pelliot*, Pel. Mi., Musée national des arts asiatiques (Musée Guimet), Paris, box 79. Translations are my own.

22 Stein Papers, Bodleian Library, Oxford University, MS 341–2.
23 Ibid.
24 Ibid.
25 Ibid. This passage from Dai Chengmo's letter was translated with the generous assistance of Ely Finch.
26 Wang Jiqing, 'Sitanyin deng ren zai Zhongguo gan le xie shenme?' [What did Stein and others really do in China?], *Lishi pinglun*, V (2022), pp. 31–7. Translation is my own.
27 Jacobs, *The Compensations of Plunder*, p. 110.
28 Papers of Roy Chapman Andrews, American Museum of Natural History, New York, C446, 1921–30, box 5, folder 18.
29 Reid, *Whose Pharaohs?*, pp. 55–6.
30 Wendy M. K. Shaw, *Possessors and Possessed: Museums, Archaeology, and the Visualization of History in the Late Ottoman Empire* (Berkeley, CA, 2003), pp. 83–107. For Osman's critiques of Islam and his caricatured 'Orientalist' paintings of Islamic subject-matter, see Edhem Eldem, 'Making Sense of Osman Hamdi Bey and His Paintings', *Muqarnas*, XXIX (2012), pp. 339–83.
31 The story of Schliemann's dig at Troy and the complicated aftermath is told in Susan Heuck Allen, *Finding the Walls of Troy: Frank Calvert and Heinrich Schliemann at Hisarlik* (Berkeley, CA, 1999).
32 The obstruction of Western archaeologists in the Near and Middle East during the 1920s and '30s is told in James F. Goode, *Negotiating for the Past: Archaeology, Nationalism, and Diplomacy in the Middle East, 1919–1941* (Austin, TX, 2007).
33 For the Chinese obstruction of Warner and Stein – among others – see Jacobs, *The Compensations of Plunder*.

CONCLUSION

1 Diyin Lu, 'Seizing Civilization: Antiquities in Shanghai's Custody, 1949–1966', PhD dissertation, Harvard University, April 2012.

SELECT BIBLIOGRAPHY

Allen, Susan Heuck, *Finding the Walls of Troy: Frank Calvert and Heinrich Schliemann at Hisarlik* (Berkeley, CA, 1999)

Brookes, Adam, *Fragile Cargo: The World War II Race to Save the Treasures of China's Forbidden City* (New York, 2023)

Chiang, Nicole T. C., *Emperor Qianlong's Hidden Treasures: Reconsidering the Collection of the Qing Imperial Household* (Hong Kong, 2019)

Colla, Elliott, *Conflicted Antiquities: Egyptology, Egyptomania, Egyptian Modernity* (Durham, NC, 2007)

Cuno, James, *Who Owns Antiquity? Museums and the Battle over Our Ancient Heritage* (Princeton, NJ, 2008)

Ebrey, Patricia Buckley, *Accumulating Culture: The Collections of Emperor Huizong* (Seattle, WA, 2008)

Galambos, Imre, 'A Forgotten Chinese Translation of the Preliminary Report of Aurel Stein's First Expedition', in *Dunhuang Studies: Prospects and Problems for the Coming Second Century of Research*, ed. Irina Popova and Liu Yi (St Petersburg, 2012), pp. 55–8

Goode, James F., *Negotiating for the Past: Archaeology, Nationalism, and Diplomacy in the Middle East, 1919–1941* (Austin, TX, 2007)

Hagen, Fredrik, and Kim Ryholt, *The Antiquities Trade in Egypt, 1880–1930: The H. O. Lange Papers* (Copenhagen, 2016)

Hevia, James L., 'Looting and Its Discontents: Moral Discourse and the Plunder of Beijing, 1900–1901', in *The Boxers, China and the World*, ed. Robert A. Bickers and R. G. Tiedemann (Lanham, MD, 2007)

Hopkirk, Peter, *Foreign Devils on the Silk Road: The Search for the Lost Cities and Treasures of Central Asia* (Amherst, MA, 1980)

Hume, Ivor Noël, *Belzoni: The Giant Archaeologists Love to Hate* (Charlottesville, VA, 2011)

Jacobs, Justin M., *Indiana Jones in History: From Pompeii to the Moon* (n.p., 2017)

—, *The Compensations of Plunder: How China Lost Its Treasures* (Chicago, IL, 2020)

James, T.G.H., *Howard Carter: The Path to Tutankhamun* (London, 2001)

Leff, Lisa Moses, *The Archive Thief: The Man Who Salvaged French Jewish History in the Wake of the Holocaust* (Oxford, 2015)

McClellan, Andrew, *Inventing the Louvre: Art, Politics, and the Origins of the Modern Museum in Eighteenth-Century Paris* (Cambridge, 1994)

Meyer, Karl E., and Shareen Blair Brysac, *The China Collectors: America's Century-Long Hunt for Asian Art Treasures* (New York, 2015)

Miles, Margaret, *Art as Plunder: The Ancient Origins of Debate about Cultural Property* (Cambridge, 2008)

Moser, Stephanie, *Wondrous Curiosities: Ancient Egypt at the British Museum* (Chicago, IL, 2006)

Netting, Lara Jaishree, *A Perpetual Fire: John C. Ferguson and His Quest for Chinese Art and Culture* (Hong Kong, 2013)

Parslow, Christopher Charles, *Rediscovering Antiquity: Karl Weber and the Excavation of Herculaneum, Pompeii, and Stabiae* (Cambridge, 1995)

Reid, Donald Malcolm, *Whose Pharaohs? Archaeology, Museums, and Egyptian National Identity from Napoleon to World War I* (Berkeley, CA, 2002)

Shaw, Wendy M. K., *Possessors and Possessed: Museums, Archaeology, and the Visualization of History in the Late Ottoman Empire* (Berkeley, CA, 2003)

St Clair, William, *Lord Elgin and the Marbles: The Controversial History of the Parthenon Sculptures* (Oxford, 1998)

Thompson, Erin L., *Possession: The Curious History of Private Collectors from Antiquity to the Present* (New Haven, CT, 2016)

Tseng, Alice Y., *The Imperial Museums of Meiji Japan: Architecture and the Art of the Nation* (Seattle, WA, 2008)

Van Tilburg, Jo Anne, *Remote Possibilities: Hoa Hakananai'a and HMS 'Topaze' on Rapa Nui* (London, 2006)

Walker, Annabel, *Aurel Stein: Pioneer of the Silk Road* (London, 1995)

Wang, Dong, *Longmen's Stone Buddhas and Cultural Heritage: When Antiquity Met Modernity in China* (Lanham, MD, 2020)
Wilkinson, Toby, *A World Beneath the Sands: The Golden Age of Egyptology* (New York, 2020)

ACKNOWLEDGEMENTS

The idea for this book arose in the course of teaching HIST 265: History of Archaeological Expeditions' at my home institution of American University. The many bright students who have taken this class over the past decade have kept me on my intellectual toes, forcing me to question whether or not the forces that constrained and enabled Western archaeologists were also responsible for the activities of dealers, diplomats and soldiers. It has been my good fortune to have the privilege of debating these fine distinctions with intelligent young minds who will not settle for broad generalizations or historical caricatures, and I look forward to many more years of the same. In addition, I am grateful to my teaching assistant Libby Tyson for always keeping a vigilant eye out for theoretical inconsistencies and empirical blind spots in my lectures.

Renee Chiang of the Oriental Ceramic Society was instrumental in introducing me to the mysterious world of dealers and identifying sources in Chinese that helped to shed an insider's perspective on their networks and supply chains. I simply could not have written the chapter on dealers without her insights and suggestions for further reading. I am also grateful to Julia Lovell, Foong Ping, Judd Kinzley, Eric Schluessel, Adam Brookes, Shao-yun Yang, David Graff, Zhu Yuqi, Jeremy Murray and Elaine Buck for stimulating discussions, answers to random queries and invitations to speak on these subjects to larger audiences. All English translations from Paul Pelliot's diary and letters in French were completed by Shilah Marks. Responsibility for the final interpretation of all topics in this book rests with me alone.

Last but not least, I would like to thank my editor Michael Leaman at Reaktion Books, who reached out to enquire about the possibility of a book on the history of plunder and ended up with one with a question mark in the title. Perhaps most importantly, when the inevitable fatigue with museum and restitution controversies began to set in, he was able to revive my enthusiasm for the project.

PHOTO ACKNOWLEDGEMENTS

The author and publishers wish to express their thanks to the sources listed below for illustrative material and/or permission to reproduce it. Some locations of artworks are also given below, in the interest of brevity:

American School of Classical Studies at Athens (Archives, Carl W. Blegen Papers): p. 171; Archives of the British Academy, London: pp. 151, 154; © The British Library Board, London (photo 392/28(794)r): p. 156; Brooklyn Museum, NY: p. 165; The Cleveland Museum of Art, OH: p. 40; from Robert de Rustafjaell, *The Light of Egypt, from Recently Discovered Predynastic and Early Christian Records* (London, 1909): p. 92; from Edward Dodwell, *Views in Greece* (London, 1821): p. 34; Flickr: pp. 38 (photo Shadowgate, CC BY 2.0), 116 (photo Gary Todd, public domain), 180 (photo Bill-Chiang, CC BY-SA 2.0); © Griffith Institute, University of Oxford: p. 15; Hearst Castle, San Simeon, CA: p. 62; Houghton Library, Harvard University, Cambridge, MA: p. 126; from *Illustrated London News*, XLIV/1265 (25 June 1864): p. 43; The J. Paul Getty Museum, Los Angeles: p. 97; photos Justin M. Jacobs: pp. 22, 31; Library of Congress, Prints and Photographs Division, Washington, DC: pp. 55, 86, 88, 136, 175; The Metropolitan Museum of Art, New York: pp. 9, 102, 104, 123; Museum für Asiatische Kunst, Staatliche Museen zu Berlin: p. 137; National Library of China, Beijing, photo World Digital Library: p. 99; National Museum of Asian Art Archives, Smithsonian Institution, Washington, DC (The Loo Family Photographs, FSA_A2010.07_02): p. 112; National Palace Museum, Taipei: p. 80; The New York Public Library: pp. 41, 44, 84; Packard Humanities Institute, Los Altos, CA: p. 36; The Palace Museum, Beijing: p. 69; from Paul Pelliot, 'Trois ans dans la haute Asie', *L'Illustration*, LXVIII/3498

(12 March 1910): p. 14; Royal Geographical Society, London: p. 78; from Heinrich Schliemann, *Ilios, ville et pays des Troyens* (Paris, 1885), photo Robarts Library, University of Toronto: p. 170; from Aurel Stein, *Ruins of Desert Cathay*, vol. I (London, 1912), photo Princeton Theological Seminary Library, NJ: p. 139; from Aurel Stein, *Ruins of Desert Cathay*, vol. II (London, 1912), photos Princeton Theological Seminary Library, NJ: pp. 46, 47, 143; from Aurel Stein, *Serindia: Detailed Report of Explorations in Central Asia and Westernmost China*, vol. IV (Oxford, 1921), photo National Institute of Informatics – Digital Silk Road Project/Digital Archive of Toyo Bunko Rare Books: p. 155; Wellcome Collection, London: p. 133; Wikimedia Commons: pp. 26 (photo Øyvind Holmstad, CC BY-SA 4.0), 120 (photo SnowFire, CC BY 4.0 – Penn Museum, Philadelphia, PA).

INDEX

Page numbers in *italics* refer to illustrations